The King is Coming

Old Testament prophesies fulfilled in Jesus the Messiah/ Christ illustrated for children and adults.

Bonnie Gay Patterson

SON OF
GOD

JESUS
OF NAZARETH
KING OF THE JEWS

OLD TESTAMENT   MEDIATOR   NEW TESTAMENT
MESSIAH

REDEEMER

LAMB
OF
GOD

SUFFERING
SERVANT

THE WAY
THE TRUTH
THE LIFE

PRINCE
OF
PEACE

MIGHTY
GOD

EVERLASTING
FATHER

HOLY ONE
OF ISRAEL

IMMANUEL

SON OF
MAN

WestBow Press books may be ordered through booksellers or by contacting:

WestBow Press
A Division of Thomas Nelson
1663 Liberty Drive
Bloomington, IN 47403
www.westbowpress.com
1-(866) 928-1240

Because of the dynamic nature of the Internet, any web addresses or links contained in this book may have changed since publication and may no longer be valid. The views expressed in this work are solely those of the author and do not necessarily reflect the views of the publisher, and the publisher hereby disclaims any responsibility for them.

Any people depicted in stock imagery provided by Thinkstock are models, and such images are being used for illustrative purposes only.

Certain stock imagery © Thinkstock.

ISBN: 978-1-4497-1450-5 (sc)
ISBN: 978-1-4497-1451-2 (e)

Library of Congress Control Number: 2011925491

Printed in the United States of America

WestBow Press rev. date: 6/2/2011

Dedicated to the memory of my husband, Gregory Patterson USMC. Greg paid for the contract to print THE KING IS COMING but did not live long enough to see it in book form. Greg passed away November 10, 2010 [Marine Corps Birthday] of cancer of the lungs, brain and bone due to exposure to Agent Orange during his time in Vietnam as a combat Marine. Greg loved God, his family and friends, his nation and other veterans. For many years he played "Taps" at military funerals in Clay, Leslie, Laurel and Pulaski counties in southeast Kentucky. When the Bible speaks of the men that went to war for Israel it calls them "valiant men." I was blessed to be married to such a man and to have met so many through him. God bless all those that serve the United States of America with honor and dignity both here in our local governments and wherever they are stationed throughout the world.

HISTORICAL TIMELINE

70AD Jerusalem destroyed; all genealogy records destroyed except those in the Bible

30AD Jesus' second Judean ministry; Crucifixion and Resurrection

27-29 Jesus' Galilean ministry

27AD Jesus' first Judean ministry

25-27 John the Baptist's ministry

4-5BC Jesus is born in Bethlehem

420BC Malachi's ministry

424BC Artaxerxes Longimanus ends his reign in Persia

425-444BC Events of book of Nehemiah

443BC Jerusalem walls reconstructed

444BC Nehemiah leads a group of returnees; Decree in Nehemiah 2

458BC Ezra leads a group of returnees

457BC Decree of Artaxerxes in Ezra 7:7-28

464BC Artaxerxes Longimanus begins to reign in Persia

483-473BC Events of book of Esther

485-465BC Ahasuerus [also know as Xerxes 1] reigns in Persia

486BC Darius 1 ends 34 year reign in Persia

515BC Temple in Jerusalem completed

519BC Darius 1 issues his decree in Ezra 6:1-12

520BC Haggai and Zechariah begin to prophesy

521BC Darius 1 begins his reign in Persia

530BC Cyrus ends his reign in Persia

536BC Temple in Jerusalem begins to be rebuilt and completed 21 years later

537BC Daniel is thrown into the lion's den: Daniel 6

538BC Decree of Cyrus at Ezra 1:1-4; Zerubbabel leads first return of Jews to Judea

539BC Cyrus conquers Babylon; events of Daniel 5 occur

559BC Cyrus begins his reign in Persia

580BC Daniels' 3 friends survive the fiery furnace: Daniel 3

586BC Jerusalem and the Temple destroyed; Judah is taken captive by the Babylonians; Obadiah writes his book

593-571BC Ezekiel writes his book

600 or 830BC Joel writes his book

603BC Daniel interprets the king's dream: Daniel 2-4

605BC Nebuchadnezzar takes Daniel and many others captive to Babylon

607-620BC Prophets Zephaniah, Habakkuk and Nahum write their books

626-584BC Jeremiah writes his books of Jeremiah and Lamentations

680-760BC Prophets Isaiah, Micah, Jonah, Amos, Hosea

930BC Nation of Israel divides into Kingdom of Judah and Kingdom of Israel

930-970BC Solomon reigns over the whole Kingdom

970-1010BC David reigns

l010-1050BC Saul, the first king, reigns

1049-1375BC Judges rule in Israel

1380-1405BC Joshua leads in conquest of Canaan and apportioning the land

1406-1730BC Events of Exodus, Leviticus, Numbers, and Deuteronomy are recorded

1805-2167BC through undateable events in book of Genesis

INTRODUCTION

Proverbs 30:4
"Who has ascended into heaven, or descended?
Who has gathered the wind in His fists?
Who has bound the waters in a garment?
Who has established all the ends of the earth?
What is His name, and what is His Son's name,
If you know?"

From the book of Genesis through Malachi prophesies of the coming Messiah [anointed one] proclaimed his uniqueness. The Old Testament pointed forward to that One that would bring salvation and release from sin and death. The New Testament pointed to Jesus as the One that the prophets, through the inspiration of the Holy Spirit, had described. This book is dedicated to clearly putting together the prophecy and the fulfillment in an easy to understand format for adults and children.

Isaiah 46:9-10 "Remember the former things of old, for I am God, and there is no other; I am God, and there is none like Me, <u>declaring the end from the beginning, and from ancient times things that are not yet done</u>, saying, 'My counsel shall stand, and I will do all My pleasure.'" Underline added for emphasis.

For a more in-depth study the book "MESSIAH IN BOTH TESTAMENTS" by Fred John Meldau can be down loaded from the Internet.

The dates for the timeline, prophesies and lives of the prophets were taken from Nelson's NKJV Study Bible, copyright 1997 by Thomas Nelson, Inc. The study aids in that Bible and the NEW OPEN BIBLE study edition also by Thomas Nelson, Inc. copyright 1990, plus "100 Prophecies Fulfilled By Jesus" by Rose Publications were invaluable.

Thanks to Bob Gass Ministries
P.O. Box 5130, Alpheretta, GA 30023
for permission to use excerpts from *The Word For You Today*

TO PARENTS, GRANDPARENTS, FOSTER PARENTS AND TEACHERS

Children have an amazing ability to learn. By the age of four they have learned a language in some cases more than one. Timothy knew the Holy Scriptures from childhood [2 Timothy 3:15] having been taught by his mother and grandmother [2 Timothy 1:5]. Jesus said "Let the little children come to Me, and do not forbid them; for of such is the kingdom of God." [Mark l0:14b]

It is a great privilege and responsibility to teach children, as they are our heritage, a gift and reward from God. [From Psalm 127:3]

"Fulfilled Prophecy Is unique to the Bible

The fact of fulfilled prophecy is found in the Bible alone; hence, it presents proof of Divine inspiration that is positive, conclusive, overwhelming. Here is the argument in brief: no man, unaided by Divine inspiration, foreknows the future, for it is an impenetrable wall, a true 'iron curtain,' to all mankind. Only an almighty and an all- knowing God can infallibly predict the future. If then one can find true prophecy (as one does in the Bible), with definite fulfillment, with sufficient time intervening between the prediction and the fulfillment, and with explicit details in the prediction to assure that the prophecies are not clever guesses, then the case is perfect and unanswerable. Remember, there were 400 years between the last of the Messianic predictions of the Old Testament and their fulfillment in the Christ of the Gospels. Many prophecies are of course much older than 400 B.C. During the period of 1100 years, from the age of Moses (1500 B.C.) to that of Malachi (400 B.C.), a succession of prophets arose, Messianic prediction took form, and all of them testified of the Messiah who was to come.

So minute and so voluminous are these Old Testament predictions and so complete is their fulfillment in the New Testament, that Dr. A.T. Pierson says, 'There would be no honest infidel in the world were Messianic prophecy studied.. .nor would there be any doubting disciples if this fact of prediction and fulfillment were fully understood.' 'And,' he continues, 'the sad fact is, we have yet to meet the first honest skeptic or critic who has carefully studied the prophecies which center in Christ' (Many Infallible Proofs)." From MESSIAH IN BOTH TESTAMENTS pages 5 and 6.

It is my desire that the following pages will help you to "always be ready to give a defense to everyone who asks you a reason for the hope that is in you" [1 Peter 3:15].

TO THE CHILDREN

There were no pictures painted of the people in the Bible and cameras have been around for less than 200 years. I have drawn what I imagine the people could have looked like and dressed like. Customs were different than ours but the basic desires of people throughout the centuries and in our time are still the same. We all desire good health, eternal life, peace, justice, safety and security. We want our loved ones to live forever and our pets too. We all look for a SUPER HERO to right the wrongs and punish the bad guys. Jesus the Christ is more than a super hero! It is my desire that as you read this book and LOOK UP THE SCRIPTURES IN YOUR OWN BIBLE you will come to a greater faith in God, His word and the ONE He sent forth.

PUZZLE

If you enjoy putting puzzles together think of the prophesies [the scriptures in the Bible written hundreds of years before Jesus was born] as pieces of a puzzle that when connected form a picture of the ONE we are to follow, believe in and know as our redeemer [the hero that brings us eternal life].

MYSTERY

If you love to read a good mystery think of the Bible as a book of clues that lead to the ONE AND ONLY hope for all of the people on earth. If you like to find out how it all ends before you read the whole book read Genesis chapters 1-3 to see how it all began and Revelation chapters 20-22 to see the end of all evil and our hope for eternity.

LOVE LETTERS

If you are a teenager and have received a love letter from someone you love think of the Bible as Gods' love letter to you. The pages are full of His love, compassion, forgiveness and promises for our future. "For God so loved the world that He gave His only begotten Son, that whoever believes in Him should not perish but have everlasting life. For God did not send His Son into the world to condemn the world, but that the world through Him might be saved." [John 3:16-17]

Just like any other love letter we need and want to read it over and over again to feel closer to the one who wrote it and sent it.

THE FIRST PROPHESY OF JESUS
FORETOLD

When Adam and Eve sinned against God in the Garden of Eden and ate of the forbidden fruit He pronounced judgment on them and the serpent [Satan] that deceived Eve. Genesis 3:15 is the first prophesy of the promised Seed giving all of mankind hope for the future.

Genesis 3:15 *"And I will put enmity between you and the woman, and between your seed and her Seed*; <u>He shall bruise your head</u> and **you shall bruise His heel**."

Adam and Eve were no doubt relieved that they would not die immediately. The seed, or child, of the woman would receive a painful bruise to his heel but he would inflict a severe blow to the head of the serpent. [Italics, bold print and underlining added to emphasize the fulfillment of the prophecy].

FULFILLED

GALATIANS 4:4 "But when the fullness of the time had come, *God sent forth His Son, born of a woman*, under the law."

Romans 16:20 "<u>And the God of peace will crush Satan under your feet shortly</u>. The grace of our Lord Jesus Christ be with you. Amen."

Hebrews 2:14 "Inasmuch then as the children have partaken of flesh and blood, He Himself likewise shared in the same, **that through death** <u>He might destroy him who had the power of death, that is, the devil."</u>

1 John 3:8 "He who sins is of the devil, for the devil has sinned from the beginning. <u>For this purpose the Son of God was manifested, that He might destroy the works of the devil."</u>

CHAPTER 1: THE BIRTH OF THE KING

FORETOLD
BORN OF A VIRGIN

Isaiah prophesized from 740 B.C. to around 681 B.C.
Isaiah 7:14 "Therefore the Lord Himself will give you a sign: Behold, the virgin shall conceive and bear a Son, and shall call His name Immanuel." Immanuel when translated literally is God-With-Us.

FULFILLED

Luke 1:26-27, 30-35 "Now in the sixth month the angel Gabriel was sent by God to a city of Galilee named Nazareth, to a virgin betrothed to a man whose name was Joseph, of the house of David. The virgin's name was Mary...Then the angel said to her, 'Do not be afraid, Mary, for you have found favor with God. And behold, you will conceive in your womb and bring forth a Son, and shall call His name JESUS. He will be great, and will be called the Son of the Highest; and the Lord God will give Him the throne of His father David. And He will reign over the house of Jacob forever, and of His kingdom there will be no end.'

Then Mary said to the angel, 'How can this be, since I do not know a man?'

And the angel answered and said to her, 'The Holy Spirit will come upon you, and the power of the Highest will overshadow you; therefore, also, that Holy One who is to be born will be called the Son of God.'

Matthew 1:22-23 "So all this was done that it might be fulfilled which was spoken by the Lord through the prophet, saying: 'Behold, the virgin shall be with child, and bear a Son, and they shall call His name Immanuel,' which is translated, 'God with us.'"

THE GENEALOGY OF JESUS

THROUGH ABRAHAM Genesis 12:la and 3 "Now the LORD said to Abram [Abraham].....I will bless those who bless you, and I will curse him who curses you; and in you all the families of the earth shall be blessed." See also Genesis 18:17-18; 22:18; 26:4; 28:14 note that ALL the families of the earth and ALL the nations were to be blessed through him.

THROUGH ISAAC Genesis 17:19 "Then God said, 'No, Sarah your wife shall bear you a son, and you shall call his name Isaac; I will establish My covenant with him for an everlasting covenant, and with his descendants after him.'" See also 21:12; 26:2-5.

THROUGH JACOB Genesis 28:13-14 [speaking to Jacob, verse 10]: "And behold, the LORD stood above it and said: 'I am the LORD God of Abraham your father and the God of Isaac; the land on which you lie I will give to you and your descendants. Also your descendants shall be as the dust of the earth; you shall spread abroad to the west and the east, to the north and the south; and in you and in your seed all the families of the earth shall be blessed.'" See also Numbers 24:17.

THROUGH JUDAH Genesis 49:10 "The scepter shall not depart from Judah, nor a lawgiver from between his feet, until Shiloh comes; and to Him shall be the obedience of the people." Shiloh means tranquil and is a descriptive quality of the Messiah or Christ.

THROUGH DAVID Isaiah 9:7 "Of the increase of His government and peace there will be no end, upon the throne of David and over His kingdom, to order it and establish it with judgment and justice from that time forward, even forever. The zeal of the LORD of hosts will perform this." See also Jeremiah 23:5; 30:9.

FULFILLED

Matthew 1:1-2 "The book of the genealogy of Jesus Christ, the son of David the Son of Abraham: Abraham begot Isaac, Isaac begot Jacob, and Jacob begot Judah and his brothers."

Verse 16 "And Jacob begot Joseph the husband of Mary, of whom was born Jesus who is called Christ."

Matthew gave Jesus' Genealogy through Joseph, the husband of Mary, even though he was not the father of Jesus. Verse 18: "Now the birth of Jesus Christ was as follows: After His mother Mary was betrothed to Joseph, before they came together, she was found with child of the Holy Spirit."

Luke gives Jesus' Genealogy through Mary so that both she and Joseph are shown to be of the proper lineage.

Luke 3:31 ....the son of David, 33...the son of Judah, 34 the son of Jacob, the son of Isaac, the son of Abraham..." But Luke goes all the way back to "Adam, the son of God." [Verse 38] which takes us back to the first prophesy at Genesis 3: 15.

NOTE

"During the life of Jesus, no one offered to dispute the well known fact that He was of the house and lineage of David, because it was in the public records that all had access to.

Since 70 A.D., when Israel's genealogical records, except those in the Bible, were destroyed or confused, **no pretending Messiah can prove he is the son of David as prophecy demands.** In other words, Messiah **had** to come before 70 A.D." MESSIAH IN BOTH TESTAMENTS by Fred John Meldau page 25.

GENEALOGY OF JESUS

[Joseph husband of] Mary mother of Jesus
Heli [grandfather]
Matthat [great-grandfather]
Levi [great-great-grandfather]
Melchi

LUKE 3:23-38   MATTHEW 1:2-26

Janna
Joseph
Mattathiah
Amos
Nahum
Esli
Naggai
Maath
Mattathiah
Semei
Joseph   Joseph [husband of Mary] step-father
Judah   Jacob [grandfather]
Joannas   Matthan [great grandfather]
Rhesa   Eleazar [great-great grandfather]
Zerubbabel   Eliud
Shealtiel   Achim
Neri   Zadok
Melchi   Azor
Addi   Eliakim
Cosam   Abiud
Elmodam   Zerubbabel
Er   Shealiel
Jose   Jeconiah
Eliezer   Josiah
Jorim   Amon
Matthat   Manasseh   Josiah begins to reign in Judah 640 BC
Levi   Hezekiah
Simeon   Ahaz   Manasseh begin to reign in Judah 697 BC
Judah   Jotham
Joseph   Uzziah
Jonan   Joram
Eliakim   Jehoshaphat
Melea   Asa
Menan   Abijah
Mattathah   Rehoboam   Solomon dies and the kingdom divides 930 BC
Nathan [mother: Bathsheba] Solomon   David dies Solomon becomes king 970BC

1018BC Samuel anoints David as king; 1003 BC David reigns over all Isreal   David
Jesse
[mother: Ruth] Obed
[mother: Rahab] Boaz
Salmon
Nahshon
Amminadab
Ram
Hezron
[mother: Tamar] Perez
Judah

2006 BC Jacob born to Isaac and Rebecca   Jacob
2066 BC Isaac born to Abraham and Sarah   Isaac
2167 BC Abraham born in Er of the Chaldeans   Abraham
Terah
Nahor
Serug
Reu
Peleg
Eber
Shelah
Cainan
Arphaxad
Shem
[The Flood] Noah
Lamech
Methuselah
Enoch
Jared
Mahalalel
Cainan
Enosh
Seth
Adam
Son of God

3

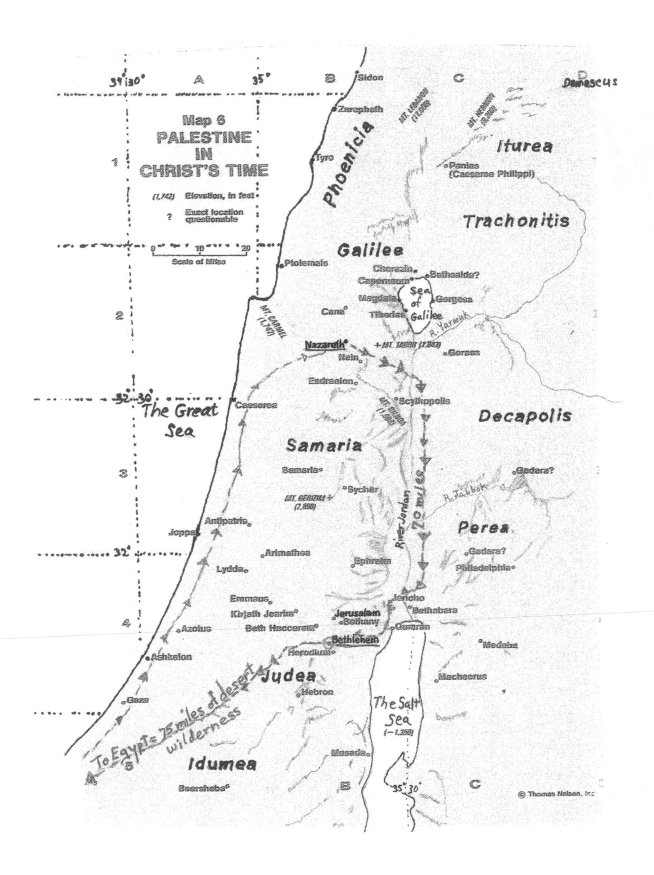

Map 6
PALESTINE
IN
CHRIST'S TIME

(1,742) Elevation, in feet
? Exact location questionable

0   10   20
Scale of Miles

Phoenicia

Iturea

Trachonitis

Galilee

Sidon
Zarephath
Tyre
Ptolemais
Chorazin
Capernaum
Bethsaida?
Magdala
Sea of Galilee
Gergesa
Cana
Tiberias
R. Yarmuk
Nazareth
+ MT. TABOR (1,843)
Nain
Gerasa
Esdraelon
The Great Sea
Caesarea
Scythopolis
Decapolis
Samaria
MT. GERIZIM +
(2,890)
Samaria
Sychar
R. Jabbok
Gadara?
Antipatris
Perea
Joppa
River Jordan
70 Mi/68
Arimathea
Gadara?
Lydda
Philadelphia
Ephraim
Emmaus
Jericho
Kirjath Jearim
Jerusalem
Bethabara
Azotus
Beth Haccerem
Bethany
Qumran
Medeba
Bethlehem
Ashkelon
Herodium
Machaerus
To Egypt is 75 miles of desert wilderness
Judea
Hebron
The Salt Sea (-1,300)
Gaza
Idumea
Masada
Beersheba

© Thomas Nelson, Inc.

BORN IN BETHLEHEM
FORETOLD

Micah prophesized between 752-699 B.C.

Micah 5:2 "But you, Bethlehem Ephrathah, though you are little among the thousands of Judah, yet out of you shall come forth to Me the One to be ruler in Israel, whose goings forth are from of old, from everlasting."

FULFILLED

Luke 2:4-7 'Joseph also went up from Galilee, out of the city of Nazareth, into Judea, to the city of David, which is called Bethlehem, because he was of the house and lineage of David, to be registered with Mary, his betrothed wife, who was with child. So it was, that while they were there, the days were completed for her to be delivered. And she brought forth her firstborn Son, and wrapped Him in swaddling cloths, and laid Him in a manger, because there was no room for them in the inn."

A BLESSING TO ALL PEOPLE
FORETOLD

Genesis 12:1a, 3b: "Now the LORD had said to Abram [Abraham]' And in you <u>all the families of the earth shall be blessed</u>.'" [Underlining added for emphasis].

FULFILLED

Luke 2:8-1 4:"Now there were in the same country shepherds living out in the fields, keeping watch over their flock by night. And behold, an angel of the Lord stood before them, and the glory of the Lord shone around them, and they were greatly afraid. Then the angel said to them, 'Do not be afraid, for behold, I bring you good tidings of great joy which will be <u>to all people</u>. For there is born to you this day in the city of David a Savior, who is Christ the Lord. And this will be the sign to you: You will find a Babe wrapped in swaddling cloths, lying in a manger.'

And suddenly there was with the angel a multitude of the heavenly host praising God and saying 'Glory to God in the highest, and on earth peace, goodwill toward men!'"

THE TIME FOR MESSIAH THE PRINCE TO APPEAR FORETOLD

Daniel composed his book around 530 B.C.

Daniel 9:25-26a "Know therefore and understand, that from the going forth of the command to restore and build Jerusalem until Messiah the Prince, there shall be seven weeks and sixty-two weeks; the street shall be built again, and the wall, even in troublesome times. And after the sixty-two weeks Messiah shall be cut off, but not for Himself; and the people of the prince who is to come shall destroy the city and the sanctuary."

7+62=69x7=483 years from the command to rebuild Jerusalem until Messiah. Numbers 14:34 God punished the Israelites one year for each day they spied out the land. Ezekiel 4:4-6 ".....I have laid on you a day for each year."

Luke 3:23a "Now Jesus Himself began His ministry at about thirty years of age,.." but He was born King of the Jews [Matthew 2:2], it is unclear whether the 483 years refers to His birth or His ministry but doing the math His ministry would be the decree of Artaxerxes [see (3) below].

THE NELSON STUDY BIBLE page 1437 "9:25 **The command to restore and build Jerusalem** may be a reference to (1) the decree of Cyrus in Ezra 1, (2) the decree of Darius in Ezra 6, (3) the decree of Artaxerxes in Ezra 7, or (4) the decree of Artaxerxes in Neh.2."

(1) Cyrus reigned in Persia from 559-530B.C., conquered Babylon in 539B.C. and returned Jews with his decree in 538B.C. Ezra 1:1-4

(2) Darius I reigned from 521-486B.C., his decree is in Ezra 6:1-12

(3) Artaxerxes reigned from 464-424B.C. and issued his decree in his seventh year, 457B.C., recorded in Ezra 7:7-28.

(4) In the twentieth year of King Artaxerxes, 444B.C., Nehemiah was sent to Jerusalem to rebuild the wall with letters in hand for the materials needed.

1st Decree	2nd Decree	3rd Decree	4th Decree	Jesus born	Jesus begins His ministry
538BC	519BC	457BC	444BC	5-4BC	26-27AD

483 years: Jesus the Messiah begins to preach

FULFILLED

Luke 2:1-2 "And it came to pass in those days that a decree went out from Caesar Augustus that all the world should be registered. This census first took place while Quirinius was governing Syria."

Luke 3:23a "Now Jesus Himself began His ministry at about thirty years of age,.."

THE NELSON STUDY BIBLE page 1567 places the birth of Jesus in 5-4B.C., the ministry of John the Baptist from 25A.D to 27A.D. The latest year that Jesus could have been baptized and start His ministry is 27A.D. For a more in-depth understanding of this prophecy see MESSIAH IN BOTH TESTAMENTS pages 32-35.

THE WISE KINGS SEEK HIM
FORETOLD

A Psalm of Solomon
Solomon reigned from 970 to 930 B.C.

Psalm 72:10,11,15 "The kings of Tarshish and of the isles will bring presents; the kings of Sheba and Seba will offer gifts. Yes, all kings shall fall down before Him; all nations shall serve Him. And He shall live; and the gold of Sheba will be given to Him; prayer also will be made for Him continually, and daily He shall be praised."

The events of Numbers took place between 1445-1405 B.C.

Numbers 24:17 "I see Him, but not now; I behold Him, but not near; A Star shall come out of Jacob; A Scepter shall rise out of Israel, And batter the brow of Moab, And destroy all the sons of tumult."

Psalm 72 and Numbers 24:15-19 are Messianic prophesies but it is unclear who these wise men from the east are. Could they be the descendants of the wise men of Babylon whose lives were spared when God revealed king Nebuchadnezzar's dream to Daniel in chapter 2 of his book? Could they be the descendants of the sons of Keturah, Abraham's second wife, whom he sent east with gifts while he was still living [Genesis 25:1-6]? Abraham certainly would have instructed all of his children, including Ishmael whom he loved dearly, of all the promises of God. Ishmael had 12 sons [Genesis 25:12- 18] "**25:18 they dwelt:** The descendants of Ishmael lived in a large area, including the Arabian Peninsula and the desert land between Canaan and Mesopotamia." [The NELSON STUDY BIBLE page 51] These are areas east of Jerusalem. Whoever they were they were looking for the Messiah-King of Israel.

FULFILLED

Matthew 2:1-3; 7-12 "Now after Jesus was born in Bethlehem of Judea in the days of Herod the king, behold, wise men from the East came to Jerusalem, saying, 'Where is He who has been born King of the Jews? For we have seen His star in the East and have come to worship Him.' When Herod the king heard this, he was troubled, and all Jerusalem with him.. .7-12 Then Herod, when he had secretly called the wise men, determined from them what time the star appeared. And he sent them to Bethlehem and said, 'Go and search carefully for the young Child, and when you have found Him, bring back word to me, that I may come and worship Him also.' When they heard the king, they departed; and behold, the star which they had seen in the East went before them, till it came and stood over where the young Child was. When they saw the star they rejoiced with exceedingly great joy. And when they had come into the house, they saw the young Child with Mary His mother, and fell down and worshiped Him. And when they had opened their treasures, they presented gifts to Him: gold, frankincense, and myrrh. Then, being divinely warned in a dream that they should not return to Herod, they departed for their own country another way."

THE FLIGHT TO EGYPT
FORETOLD

Hosea prophesied during the eighth century B.C.

Hosea 11:1 "When Israel was a child, I loved him, and out of Egypt I called My son."

FULFILLED

Matthew 2:13-15 "Now when they had departed, behold, an angel of the Lord appeared to Joseph in a dream, saying, 'Arise, take the young Child and His mother, flee to Egypt, and stay there until I bring you word; for Herod will seek the young Child to destroy Him." When he arose, he took the young Child and His mother by night and departed for Egypt, and was there until the death of Herod, that it might be fulfilled which was spoken by the Lord through the prophet, saying, 'Out of Egypt I called My Son.'"

THE SLAUGHTER OF CHILDREN
FORETOLD

Jeremiah's ministry extended from 626 to 586 B.C.

Jeremiah 31:15 "Thus says the LORD: 'A voice was heard in Ramah, lamentation and bitter weeping, Rachel weeping for her children, refusing to be comforted for her children, because they are no more.'"

God knew the evil intent of Satan and his followers and foretold what they would try to do 600 years in advance.

FULFILLED

Matthew 2:16-18 "Then Herod, when he saw that he was deceived by the wise men, was exceedingly angry; and he sent forth and put to death all the male children who were in Bethlehem and in all its districts, from two years old and under, according to the time which he had determined from the wise men. Then was fulfilled what was spoken by Jeremiah the prophet, saying: 'A voice was heard in Ramah, lamentation, weeping, and great mourning, Rachel weeping for her children, refusing to be comforted, because they are no more.'"

CHAPTER 2: THE WAY OF THE LORD PREPARED

ELIJAH AND THE PROPHETS OF BAAL
Read 1 Kings 18:20-40 and chapter 19:1-18.

GOD USES ELIJAH TO TURN ISREAL BACK TO HIM

1 Kings 18:36-39 "And it came to pass at the time of the offering of the evening sacrifice, that Elijah the prophet came near and said, 'LORD God of Abraham, Isaac, and Israel, let it be known this day that You are God in Israel and I am Your servant, and that I have done all these things at Your word. Hear me, O LORD, hear me, that this people may know that You are the LORD God, and that You have turned their hearts back to You again.'

Then the fire of the LORD fell and consumed the burnt sacrifice, and the wood and the stones and the dust, and it licked up the water that was in the trench. Now when all the people saw it, they fell on their faces; and they said, 'The LORD, He is God! The LORD, He is God!'"

PRECEDED BY ELIJAH
FORETOLD

The book of Malachi was written over 400 years before Christ.

Malachi 4:5-6 "Behold, I will send you Elijah the prophet before the coming of the great and dreadful day of the LORD. And he will turn the hearts of the fathers to the children, and the hearts of the children to their fathers, lest I come and strike the earth with a curse."

FULFILLED

When John's birth was announced to his father, Zacharias, the angel said: "He will also go before Him in the spirit and power of Elijah, 'to turn the hearts of the fathers to the children,' and the disobedient to the wisdom of the just, to make ready a people prepared for the Lord." Luke 1:17 [see all of Luke chapter 1].

Matthew 11:13-14 Jesus said: "For all the prophets and the law prophesied until John. And if you are willing to receive it, he is Elijah who is to come."

THE WAY OF THE LORD PREPARED FORETOLD

Isaiah prophesized from 740B.C. to 681B.C.

Isaiah 40:3-5 "The voice of one crying in the wilderness: 'Prepare the way of the LORD; make straight in the desert a highway for our God. Every valley shall be exalted and every mountain and hill brought low; the crooked places shall be made straight and the rough places smooth; the glory of the LORD shall be revealed, and all flesh shall see it together; for the mouth of the LORD has spoken."

The book of Malachi was written over 400 years before Christ

Malachi 3:1 "Behold, I send My messenger, and he will prepare the way before Me. And the Lord, whom you seek, will suddenly come to His temple, even the messenger of the covenant, in whom you delight. Behold, He is coming,' says the LORD of hosts."

FULFILLED

Luke 3:2b-6 "...the word of God came to John the son of Zacharias in the wilderness. And he went into all the region around the Jordan, preaching a baptism of repentance for the remission of sins, as it is written in the book of the words of Isaiah the prophet, saying: 'The voice of one crying in the wilderness: "Prepare the way of the LORD; make His paths straight. Every valley shall be filled and every mountain and hill brought low; the crooked places shall be made straight and the rough ways smooth; and all flesh shall see the salvation of God.""

Luke 7:24, 27 "When the messengers of John had departed, He began to speak to the multitudes concerning John: 'What did you go out into the wilderness to see? A reed shaken by the wind?... This is he of whom it is written: "Behold, I send My messenger before Your face, who will prepare Your way before You.""

See also Mark 1:1-8 and 9:11-13 and Matthew 11:7-10.

DECLARED THE SON OF GOD
FORETOLD

Psalm 2:7 "I will declare the decree: the LORD has said to Me, 'You are My Son, today I have begotten You.'"

Isaiah 42:1 "Behold! My Servant whom I uphold, My Elect One in whom My soul delights! I have put My Spirit upon Him; He will bring forth justice to the Gentiles."

FULFILLED

Matthew 3:13,16-17 "Then Jesus came from Galilee to John at the Jordan to be baptized by him..., When He had been baptized, Jesus came up immediately from the water; and behold, the heavens were opened to Him, and He saw the Spirit of God descending like a dove and alighting upon Him. And suddenly a voice came from heaven, saying, 'This is My beloved Son, in whom I am well pleased.'" See also Matthew 12:18; 17:5; Mark 1:1, 11; Luke 3:22; John 1:18; Hebrews 1:5; 5:5.

CHAPTER 3: HIS ANOINTED MINISTRY

ANOINTED TO PREACH LIBERTY TO THE CAPTIVES, HEAL THE BROKENHEARTED, COMFORT ALL WHO MOURN FORETOLD

Isaiah 61:1-2 "The Spirit of the Lord GOD is upon Me, because the LORD has anointed Me to preach good tidings to the poor; He has sent Me to heal the brokenhearted, to proclaim liberty to the captives, and the opening of the prison to those who are bound; to proclaim the acceptable year of the LORD, and the day of vengeance of our God; to comfort all who mourn."

FULFILLED

Luke 4:16-21 "So He came to Nazareth, where He had been brought up. And as His custom was, He went into the synagogue on the Sabbath day, and stood up to read. And He was handed the book of the prophet Isaiah. And when He had opened the book, He found the place where it was written: 'The Spirit of the LORD is upon Me, because He has anointed Me to preach the gospel to the poor; He has sent Me to heal the brokenhearted, to proclaim liberty to the captives and recovery of sight to the blind to set at liberty those who are oppressed; to proclaim the acceptable year of the LORD.' Then He closed the book, and gave it back to the attendant and sat down. And the eyes of all who were in the synagogue were fixed on Him. And He began to say to them, 'Today this Scripture is fulfilled in your hearing.'"

Acts 10:38 "how God anointed Jesus of Nazareth with the Holy Spirit and with power, who went about doing good and healing all who were oppressed by the devil, for God was with Him."

HIS MINISTRY IN ZEBULUN, NEPHTALI, AND GALILEE FORETOLD

Isaiah prophesied from 740-681B.C.

Isaiah 9:1-2 'Nevertheless the gloom will not be upon her who is distressed, as when at first He lightly esteemed the land of Zebulun and the land of Naphtali, and afterward more heavily oppressed her, by the way of the sea, beyond the Jordan, in Galilee of the Gentiles. The people who walked in darkness have seen a great light; those who dwelt in the land of the shadow of death, upon them a light has shined."

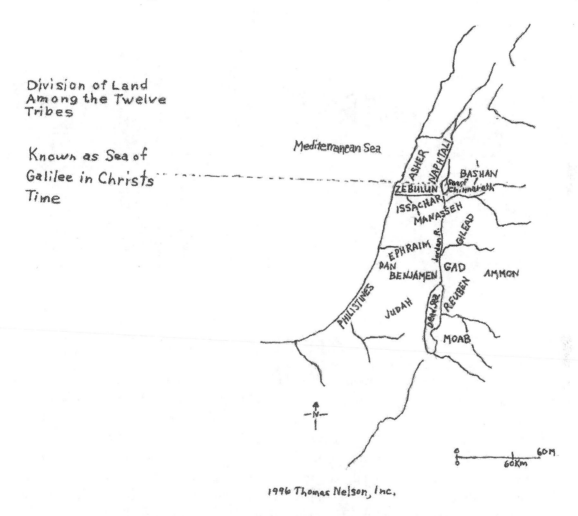

Division of Land Among the Twelve Tribes

Known as Sea of Galilee in Christs Time

1996 Thomas Nelson, Inc.

FULFILLED

Matthew 4:12-16 "Now when Jesus heard that John had been put in prison, He departed to Galilee. And leaving Nazareth, He came and dwelt in Capernaum, which is by the sea, in the regions of Zebulun and Naphtali, that it might be fulfilled which was spoken by Isaiah the prophet, saying: 'The land of Zebulun and the land of Naphtali, by the way of the sea, beyond the Jordan, Galilee of the Gentiles: The people who sat in darkness saw a great light, and upon those who sat in the region and shadow of death light has dawned.'"

SPEAKS IN PARABLES
FORETOLD

Asaph wrote Psalm 78 and many others. He was a musician during the time of kings David and Solomon.

Psalm 78:2 "I will open my mouth in a parable; I will utter dark sayings of old,"

Isaiah 6:9-10 "And He said, 'Go, and tell this people: "Keep on hearing, but do not understand; keep on seeing, but do not perceive." Make the heart of this people dull, and their ears heavy, and shut their eyes; lest they see with their eyes, and hear with their ears, and understand with their heart, and return and be healed."

FULFILLED

Matthew 13:10-17 "And the disciples came and said to Him, 'Why do You speak to them in parables?'

He answered and said to them, 'Because it has been given to you to know the mysteries of the kingdom of heaven, but to them it has not been given. For whoever has, to him more will be given, and he will have abundance; but whoever does not have, even what he has will be taken away from him. Therefore I speak to them in parables, because seeing they do not see, and hearing they do not hear, nor do they understand. And in them the prophecy of Isaiah is fulfilled, which says: "Hearing you will hear and shall not understand, and seeing you will see and not perceive; for the hearts of this people have grown dull. Their ears are hard of hearing, and their eyes they have closed, lest they should see with their eyes and hear with their ears, lest they should understand with their hearts and turn, so that I should heal them." But blessed are your eyes for they see, and your ears for they hear; for assuredly, I say to you that many prophets and righteous men desired to see what you see, and did not see it, and to hear what you hear, and did not hear it."

Matthew 13:34-35 "All these things Jesus spoke to the multitude in parables; and without a parable He did not speak to them, that it might be fulfilled which was spoken by the prophet, saying: 'I will open My mouth in parables; I will utter things kept secret from the foundation of the world." See also Mark 4:2-12, Luke 8:10.

A PARABLE IS A STORY DEALING WITH ORDINARY LIFE FROM WHICH A MORAL MESSAGE OR RELIGIOUS TRUTH IS TAUGHT.

SOME OF THE PARABLES
Which ones are pictured?

Believers Are Salt and Light: Matthew 5:13-16; see also Mark 9:50 and Luke 14:34-35.
Build on the Rock: Matthew 7:24-29; see also Luke 6:47-49.
The Sower: Matthew 13:3-9, 18-23; see also Mark 4:1-9, 13-20, Luke 8:4-8, 11-15.
The Wheat and the Tares: Matthew 13:24-30, 36-43.
The Mustard Seed: Matthew 13:31-32; see also Mark 4:30-32; Luke 13:18-19.
The Leaven: Matthew 13:33; see also Luke 13:20-21
The Hidden Treasure: Matthew 13:44.
The Pearl of Great Price: Matthew 13:45.
The Dragnet: Matthew 13:47-52.
Defilement Comes from Within: Matthew 15:1-20; see also Mark 7:1-23.
The Lost Sheep: Matthew 18:10-14; see also Luke 15:1-7.
The Unforgiving Servant: Matthew 18:21-35.
The Workers in the Vineyard: Matthew 20:1-16.
The Two Sons: Matthew 21:28-32.
The Wicked Vinedressers: Matthew 21:33-46; see also Mark 12:1-12; Luke 20:9-19.
The Wedding Feast: Matthew 22:1-14; see also Luke 14:15-24.
The Fig Tree: Matthew 24:32-35; see also Mark 13:28-31; Luke 21:29-33.
The Ten Virgins: Matthew 25:1-13.
The Talents: Matthew 25:14-30; see also Luke 19:11-27.
The Unjust Steward: Luke 16:1-13.
The Rich Man and Lazarus: Luke 16:19-31
The Persistent Widow: Luke 18:1-8.
The Pharisee and the Tax Collector: Luke 9:1-14.
Take the Lowly Place: Luke 14:7-14.
The Lost Coin: Luke 15:8-10.
The Lost Son: Luke 15:11-32.
The Rich Fool: Luke 12:16-21.
The Good Samaritan: Luke 10:25-37.

HE WOULD BE A SAVIOR, HEALER AND MIRACLE WORKER
FORETOLD

Isaiah 35:4-6 "Say to those who are fearful-hearted, 'Be strong, do not fear! Behold, your God will come with vengeance, with the recompense of God; He will come and save you.' Then the eyes of the blind shall be opened, and the ears of the deaf shall be unstopped. Then the lame shall leap like a deer, and the tongue of the dumb sing. For waters shall burst forth in the wilderness and streams in the desert."

FULFILLED

Matthew 11:2-6 "And when John had heard in prison about the works of Christ, he sent two of his disciples and said to Him, 'Are You the Coming One, or do we look for another?'

Jesus answered and said to them, 'Go and tell John the things which you hear and see: The blind see and the lame walk; the lepers are cleansed and the deaf hear; the dead are raised up and the poor have the gospel preached to them. And blessed is he who is not offended because of Me.'"

See also Matthew 9:30; 12:22; 20:33-34; 21:14; Mark 7:32-37; Luke 7:18-35; John 9:1-7; 11:47.

SOME OF THE MIRACLES OF JESUS

His first miracle was turning water into wine at a wedding feast.   John 2:1-1l

He healed a Nobleman's son.   John 4:46-54

Demoniac healed on the Sabbath Day.   Mark 1:21-28; Luke 4:31-37

Peter's Mother-in-law cured, plus others.   Matt. 8:14-17; Mark 1:20-34; Luke 4:38-41

Leper healed and the response is recorded.   Matt. 8:1-4; Mark 1:40-45; Luke 5:12-16

Paralytic healed.   Matt. 9:1-8; Mark 2:1-12; Luke 5:17-26

Heals a lame man.   Luke 5:1-47

Withered hand healed on a Sabbath.   Matt. 12:9-14; Mark 3:1-6; Luke 6:6-11

Multitudes healed by Sea of Galilee.   Matt. 12:15-21; Mark 3:7-12; Luke 6:17-19

Centurion's servant healed.   Matt. 8:5-13; Luke 7:1-10

Raises widow's son from the dead.   Luke 7:11-17

Sea of Galilee calmed.   Matt. 8:23-27; Mark 4:35-41; Luke 8:22-25

Gadarene demoniac healed.   Matt. 8:28-34; Mark 5:1-20; Luke 8:26-39

Jairus's daughter raised and woman with hemorrhage healed.   Matt. 9:18-26;Mark 5:21-43; Luke 8:40-56

Two blind men have their sight restored.   Matt. 9:27-31

Mute demoniac healed.   Matt. 9:32-34

5000 fed near Bethsaida.   Matt. 14:13-21; Mark 6:30-44; Luke 9:10-17; John 6:1-14

Jesus walks on the water.   Matt. 14:22-33; Mark 6:45-52; John 6:15-21

Sick people of Gennesaret healed.   Matt. 14:34-36; Mark 6:53-56

Syro-Phoenician's daughter healed.   Matt. 15:21-28; Mark 7:24-30

Afflicted healed at Decapolis.   Matt. 15:29-31; Mark 7:31-37

4000 fed at Decapolis.   Matt. 15:32-39; Mark 8:1-9

Blind man healed.   Matt. 16:5-12; Mark 8:14-26

Epileptic healed.   Matt. 17:14-21; Mark 9:14-29; Luke 9:27-42

Taxes paid.   Matt. 17:24-27

Man born blind healed.   John 9:1-41

Crippled woman healed on the Sabbath.   Luke 13:10-17

Man healed of dropsy on the Sabbath.   Luke 14:1-7

Lazarus resurrected after 4 days in the grave.   John 11:1-44

Heals 10 lepers.   Luke 17:12-19

Blind Bartimaeus healed.   Mark 10:46-52; Luke 18:35-43

John 21:25 "And there are also many other things that Jesus did, which if they were written one by one, I suppose that even the world itself could not contain the books that would be written. Amen."

A PROPHET LIKE MOSES
FORETOLD

Moses presented the Deuteronomy Law in 1406 B. C.

Deuteronomy 18:15-19 "The LORD your God will raise up for you a Prophet like me from your midst, from your brethren. Him you shall hear, according to all you desired of the LORD your God in Horeb in the day of the assembly, saying, 'Let me not hear again the voice of the LORD my God, nor let me see this great fire anymore, lest I die.' And the LORD said to me: 'What they have spoken is good. I will raise up for them a Prophet like you from among their brethren, and will put My words in His mouth, and He shall speak to them all that I command Him. And it shall be that whoever will not hear My words, which He speaks in My name, I will require it of him.'"

"Moses was a LAWGIVER, a LEADER, a KING (Captain), a DELIVERER, a PROPHET (God's spokesman), and an INTERCESSOR for the people, with whom **God spoke face to face**; so there arose not in Israel a prophet, like Moses (cf. Deut. 34:10-12; Numb. 12:6-8). He was the only man in Jewish history who exercised the functions of Prophet, Priest, and King in one ministry." MESSIAH in Both Testaments by Fred John Meldau, page 78.

Israelites fed by Manna in the Wilderness

Jesus feeds 5,000 with 5 barley loaves and 2 small fish

FULFILLED

Acts 3:19-24 [from Peters second sermon] "Repent therefore and be converted, that your sins may be blotted out, so that times of refreshing may come from the presence of the Lord, and that He may send Jesus Christ, who was preached to you before, whom heaven must receive until the times of restoration of all things, which God has spoken by the mouth of all His holy prophets since the world began. For Moses truly said to the fathers, 'The LORD your God will raise up for you a Prophet like me from your brethren. Him you shall hear in all things, whatever He says to you. And it shall be that every soul who will not hear that Prophet shall be utterly destroyed from among the people.' Yes, and all the prophets, from Samuel and those who follow, as many as have spoken have also foretold these days."

John 6:14 [after Jesus fed 5000] "Then those men, when they had seen the sign that Jesus did, said, 'This is truly the Prophet who is to come into the world.'"

See also Matthew 21:11; Luke 7:16; 24:19; John 7:40.

THE KING IS COMING
FORETOLD

Zechariah prophesized between 520-518B.C.

Zechariah 9:9 "Rejoice greatly, O daughter of Zion! Shout, O daughter of Jerusalem! Behold, your King is coming to you; He is just and having salvation, lowly and riding on a donkey, a colt, the foal of a donkey."

FULFILLED

Mark 11:1-10 "Now when they drew near Jerusalem, to Bethphage and Bethany, at the Mount of Olives, He sent two of His disciples; and He said to them, 'Go into the village opposite you; and as soon as you have entered it you will find a colt tied, on which no one has sat. Loose it and bring it. And if anyone says to you, "Why are you doing this?" say, "The Lord has need of it," and immediately he will send it here.'

So they went their way, and found the colt tied by the door outside on the street, and they loosed it. But some of those who stood there said to them, 'What are you doing, loosing the colt?'

And they spoke to them just as Jesus had commanded. So they let them go. Then they brought the colt to Jesus and threw their clothes on it, and He sat on it. And many spread their clothes on the road, and others cut down leafy branches from the trees and spread them on the road. Then those who went before and those who followed cried out, saying:

'Hosanna! [oh save!]

Blessed is He who comes in the name of the LORD! [Psalm 18:26]

Blessed is the kingdom of our father David

That comes in the name of the Lord!

Hosanna in the highest!"

See also Matthew 21:1-11; Luke 19:28-40; John 12:12-19.

GREAT ZEAL FOR GOD'S HOUSE
FORETOLD

A Psalm written by King David, he reigned from 1010-970B.C.

Psalm 69:9 "Because zeal for Your house has eaten me up, and the reproaches of those who reproach You have fallen on me."

Jeremiah was called to prophesy in 626B.C.

Jeremiah 7:11 "Has this house, which is called by My name, become a den of thieves in your eyes? Behold, I, even I, have seen it,' says the LORD."

Isaiah 56:7b "...For My house shall be called a house of prayer for all nations."

FULFILLED

Matthew 21:12-13 "Then Jesus went into the temple of God and drove out all those who bought and sold in the temple, and overturned the tables of the money changers and the seats of those who sold doves. And He said to them, 'It is written, "My house shall be called a house of prayer," but you have made it a "den of thieves."'"

John 2:17 "Then His disciples remembered that it was written, 'Zeal for Your house has eaten Me up.'" See also verses 13-16; Mark 11:15-17; Luke 19:45-46

CHILDREN PRAISE AND ADORE HIM FORETOLD

A Psalm of David

Psalm 8:2 "Out of the mouth of babes and nursing infants You have ordained strength, because of Your enemies, that You may silence the enemy and the avenger."

FULFILLED

Matthew 21:14-16 "Then the blind and the lame came to Him in the temple, and He healed them. But when the chief priests and scribes saw the wonderful things that He did, and the children crying out in the temple and saying, 'Hosanna to the Son of David!' they were indignant and said to Him, 'Do You hear what these are saying?' And Jesus said to them, 'Yes. Have you never read "Out of the mouth of babes and nursing infants You have perfected praise."'"

HE WILL RESTORE ISRAEL AND BECOME A LIGHT TO THE GENTILES
FORETOLD

Isaiah 49:1-6 "Listen, O coastlands, to Me, and take heed, you peoples from afar! **The LORD has called Me from the womb; from the matrix of My mother He has made mention of My name**. And He has made My mouth like a sharp sword; in the shadow of His hand He has hidden Me, and made Me a polished shaft; in His quiver He has hidden Me.'

And He said to me, 'You are My servant. O Israel, in whom I will be glorified.' Then I said. 'I have labored in vain, I have spent my strength for nothing and in vain; yet surely my just reward is with the LORD, and my work with my God.'

And now the LORD says, Who formed Me from the womb to be His Servant, to bring Jacob back to Him, so that Israel is gathered to Him (for I shall be glorious in the eyes of the LORD. and My God shall be My strength), indeed He says, 'It is too small a thing that You should be My Servant to raise up the tribes of Jacob, and to restore the preserved ones of Israel: *I will also give You as a light to the Gentiles, that You should be My salvation to the ends of the earth.*'" [Italics, bold print and underlining added for emphasis and to tie verses together.]

FULFILLED

Luke 1:30-31 "Then the angel said to her, 'Do not be afraid, Mary, for you have found favor with God. And behold, **you will conceive in your womb and bring forth a Son, and shall call His name JESUS.**'"

Matthew 23:37 "O Jerusalem, Jerusalem, the one who kills the prophets and stones those who are sent to her! How often I wanted to gather your children together, as a hen gathers her chicks under her wings, but you were not willing!"

Luke 2:30-32 *"For my eyes have seen Your salvation which You have prepared before the face of all peoples, a light to bring revelation to the Gentiles, and the glory of Your people Israel."*

THE SERVANT OF THE LORD
FORETOLD

THE ONE WHO WILL ESTABLISH JUSTICE FOR ALL

Isaiah 42:1-4 "Behold! My Servant whom I uphold, My Elect One in whom My soul delights! I have put My Spirit upon Him; <u>He will bring forth justice to the Gentiles</u>. He will not cry out, nor raise His voice, nor cause His voice to be heard in the street. A bruised reed He will not break, and smoking flax He will not quench; He will bring forth justice for truth. He will not fail nor be discouraged, till He has established justice in the earth; and the coastlands shall wait for His law."

Gentiles are anyone that is not an Israelite or Jewish by birth. Underlining added for emphasis.

FULFILLED

Matthew 12:14-21 "Then the Pharisees went out and plotted against Him, how they might destroy Him. But when Jesus knew it, He withdrew from there. And great multitudes followed Him, and He healed them all. Yet He warned them not to make Him known, that it might be fulfilled which was spoken by Isaiah the prophet, saying:

'Behold! My Servant whom I have chosen, My Beloved in whom My soul is well pleased! I will put My Spirit upon Him, and He will declare justice to the Gentiles. He will not quarrel nor cry out, nor will anyone hear His voice in the streets. A bruised reed He will not break, and smoking flax He will not quench, till He sends forth justice to victory. <u>And in His name Gentiles will trust</u>.'"

CHAPTER 4: BETRAYED

BETRAYED BY A CLOSE FRIEND FOR 30 PIECES OF SILVER FORETOLD

Psalms of King David; he reigned between 1010-970B.C.

Psalm 41:9 "Even my own familiar friend in whom I trusted, who ate my bread, has lifted up his heel against me."

Psalm 55:12-14 "For it is not an enemy who reproaches me; then I could bear it. Nor is it one who hates me who has exalted himself against me; then I could hide from him. But it was you, a man my equal, my companion and my acquaintance. We took sweet counsel together, and walked to the house of God in the throng."

Zechariah prophesized between 520-518 B.C.

Zechariah 11:12 "Then I said to them, 'If it is agreeable to you, give me my wages; and if not, refrain.' So they weighed out for my wages thirty pieces of silver."

FULFILLED

Matthew 26:14-16 "Then one of the twelve, called Judas Iscariot, went to the chief priests and said, 'What are you willing to give me if I deliver Him to you?' And they counted out to him thirty pieces of silver. So from that time he sought opportunity to betray Him."

Matthew 26:20-25 "When evening had come, He sat down with the twelve. Now as they were eating, He said, 'Assuredly, I say to you, one of you will betray Me.'

And they were exceedingly sorrowful, and each of them began to say to Him, 'Lord, is it I?'

He answered and said, 'He who dipped his hand with Me in the dish will betray Me. The Son of Man indeed goes just as it is written of Him, but woe to that man by whom the Son of Man is betrayed! It would have been good for that man if he had not been born.'

Then Judas, who was betraying Him, answered and said, 'Rabbi, is it I?'

He said to him, 'You have said it.'"

See also Mark 14:10-21; Luke 22:1-13.

DESERTED BY HIS FOLLOWERS
FORETOLD

Zechariah 13:6-7 "And one will say to him, 'What are these wounds between your arms (Or hands)?' Then he will answer, 'Those with which I was wounded in the house of my friends.'

'Awake, O sword, against My Shepherd, against the Man who is My Companion,' says the LORD of hosts. 'Strike the Shepherd, and the sheep will be scattered; then I will turn My hand against the little ones."

FULFILLED

Matthew 26:31-32,56 "Then Jesus said to them, 'All of you will be made to stumble because of Me this night, for it is written:

"I will strike the Shepherd, and the sheep of the flock will be scattered."

But after I have been raised, I will go before you to Galilee.'

56 "'But all this was done that the Scriptures of the prophets might be fulfilled.'

Then all the disciples forsook Him and fled." See also Mark 14:27; John 16:25- 33. Please read all of Matthew 26:31-75.

HE WILL BE FALSLY ACCUSED
FORETOLD

A Psalm of King David.

Psalm 109:1-5 "Do not keep silent, O God of my praise! For the mouth of the wicked and the mouth of the deceitful have opened against me; they have spoken against me with a lying tongue. They have also surrounded me with words of hatred, and fought against me without a cause. In return for my love they are my accusers, but I give myself to prayer. Thus they have rewarded me evil for good, and hatred for my love."

FULFILLED

Matthew 26:57-68 "And those who had laid hold of Jesus led Him away to Caiaphas the high priest, where the scribes and the elders were assembled. But Peter followed Him at a distance to the high priest's courtyard. And he went in and sat with the servants to see the end.

Now the chief priests, the elders, and all the council sought false testimony against Jesus to put Him to death, but found none. Even though many false witnesses came forward, they found none. But at last two false witnesses came forward and said, 'This fellow said, "I am able to destroy the temple of God and to build it in three days."'

And the high priest arose and said to Him, 'Do You answer nothing? What is it these men testify against You?' But Jesus kept silent. And the high priest answered and said to Him, 'I put You under oath by the living God: Tell us if You are the Christ, the Son of God!'

Jesus said to him, 'It is as you said. Nevertheless, I say to you, hereafter you will see the Son of Man sitting at the right hand of the Power, and coming on the clouds of heaven.'

Then the high priest tore his clothes, saying, 'He has spoken blasphemy! What further need do we have of witnesses? Look, now you have heard His blasphemy! What do you think?'

They answered and said, 'He is deserving of death.'

Then they spat in His face and beat Him; and others struck Him with the palms of their hands, saying, 'Prophesy to us, Christ! Who is the one who struck You?'"

THE FIELD OF BLOOD
FORETOLD

Zechariah 11:13 "And the LORD said to me, 'Throw it to the potter'—that princely price they set on me. So I took the thirty pieces of silver and threw them into the house of the LORD for the potter."

FULFILLED

Matthew 27:3-10 "Then Judas, His betrayer, seeing that He had been condemned, was remorseful and brought back the thirty pieces of silver to the chief priests and elders, saying, 'I have sinned by betraying innocent blood.'

And they said, 'What is that to us? You see to it!'

Then he threw down the pieces of silver in the temple and departed, and went and hanged himself.

But the chief priests took the silver pieces and said, 'It is not lawful to put them into the treasury, because they are the price of blood.' And they consulted together and bought with them the potter's field, to bury strangers in. Therefore that field has been called the Field of Blood to this day.

Then was fulfilled what was spoken by Jeremiah the prophet, saying, 'And they took the thirty pieces of silver, the value of Him who was priced, whom they of the children of Israel priced, and gave them for the potter's field, as the LORD directed me.'" See also Acts 1:16-20.

CHAPTER 5: MEDIATOR OF THE NEW COVENANT

THE NEW COVENANT
FORETOLD

Jeremiah 31:31-34 "Behold, the days are coming, says the LORD, when I will make a new covenant with the house of Israel and with the house of Judah—not according to the covenant that I made with their fathers in the day that I took them by the hand to lead them out of the land of Egypt, My covenant which they broke, though I was a husband to them, says the LORD. But this is the covenant that I will make with the house of Israel after those days, says the LORD: I will put My law in their minds, and write it on their hearts; and I will be their God, and they shall be My people. No more shall every man teach his neighbor, and every man his brother, saying, 'Know the LORD,' for they all shall know Me, from the least of them to the greatest of them, says the LORD. For I will forgive their iniquity, and their sin I will remember no more."

FULFILLED

When Jesus celebrated His last Passover with His disciples He instituted the Lord's Supper, which is the observance of the new covenant.

Matthew 26:26-29 "And as they were eating, Jesus took bread, blessed and broke it, and gave it to the disciples and said, 'Take, eat; this is My body.' Then He took the cup, and gave thanks, and gave it to them, saying, 'Drink from it, all of you. For this is My blood of the new covenant which is shed for many for the remission of sins. But I say to you, I will not drink of this fruit of the vine from now on until that day when I drink it new with you in My Father's kingdom." See also Mark 14:22-25; Luke 22:14-23; 1 Corinthians 11:23-26.

The apostles were "ministers of the new covenant not of the letter but of the Spirit; for the letter kills, but the Spirit gives life." 2 Corinthians 3:6b

Hebrews 8:7-13 "For if that first covenant had been faultless, then no place would have been sought for a second. Because finding fault with them, He says: 'Behold, the days are coming, says the LORD, when I will make a new covenant with the house of Israel and with the house of Judah—not according to the covenant that I made with their fathers in the day when I took them by the hand to lead them out of the land of Egypt; because they did not continue in My covenant, and I disregarded them, says the LORD. For this is the covenant that I will make with the house of Israel after those days, says the LORD: I will put My laws in their mind and write them on their hearts; and I will be their God, and they shall be My people. None of them shall teach his neighbor, and none his brother, saying, "Know the LORD," for all shall know Me, from the least of them to the greatest of them. For I will be merciful to their unrighteousness, and their sins and their lawless deeds I will remember no more.'

In that He says, 'A new covenant,' He has made the first obsolete. Now what is becoming obsolete and growing old is ready to vanish away." See also Hebrews 9:11-15.

JESUS: OUR MEDIATOR
FORETOLD

There is no definite date for the writing of the book of Job. The latest date suggested is during the time of Solomon [970BC-930BC] when wisdom literature flourished.

Job was arguing his case after loosing his children, his wealth and his health. He wrongfully thought all his oppression came from God and saw the need for a mediator between he and God.

Job 9:32-33 "For He is not a man, as I am, that I may answer Him, and that we should go to court together. Nor is there any mediator between us, who may lay his hand on us both."

FULFILLED

1 Timothy 2:5-6 "For there is one God and one Mediator between God and men, the Man Christ Jesus, who gave Himself a ransom for all, to be testified in due time,"

Galatians 3:19-21 "What purpose then does the law serve? It was added because of transgressions, till the Seed should come to whom the promise was made; and it was appointed through angels by the hand of a mediator. Now a mediator does not mediate for one only, but God is one. Is the law then against the promises of God? Certainly not! For if there had been a law given which could have given life, truly righteousness would have been by the law."

Hebrews 12:24 "to Jesus the Mediator of the new covenant, and the blood of sprinkling that speaks better things than that of Abel."

IDENTIFYING ONE INDIVIDUAL
OUT OF THE BILLIONS
THAT HAVE EVER LIVED

If I wanted to send anyone a letter that lived anywhere in the world I could do that. With just 7 important pieces of information on the envelope, as long as they have mail service, it would reach them.

1) Name
2) House number
3) Street name
4) City
5) State or Province
6) Zip code
7) Country

Identifying the promised ONE is so important that the Bible has given us many more than "7 important pieces of information" to find that ONE. Let's review what we have seen so far:

1) Born of a virgin
2) Of the house and lineage of King David
3) Born in Bethlehem
4) Called out of Egypt
5) Rachel weeping for her children
6) Preceded by a messenger that would prepare the way before Him
7) Declared the Son of God
8) Anointed to preach liberty
9) Speaks in parables
10) He would be a Savior, Healer and Miracle Worker
11) A prophet like Moses
12) He would have great zeal for God's House
13) Children would praise and adore Him
14) The King would come riding on a donkey
15) A light to the Gentiles, bringing salvation to the ends of the earth
16) He would be betrayed by a close friend who would sell Him out for 30 pieces of silver
17) He would establish a New Covenant and be our Mediator

We are now going into two of the most detailed of the prophecies. Jesus came to fulfill ALL the prophecies and knew in advance that He would have to suffer to redeem us from sin and death.

CHAPTER 6: THE SUFFERING SERVANT

Please read Isaiah 52:13-53:12 and remember that Isaiah wrote this 700 years before Jesus was born. These passages were not understood until Jesus fulfilled them on the cross. They are full of what seems to be contradictory statements:

1) He is a servant that is both humiliated and exalted
2) He is a root out of dry ground-yet fruitful
3) He has no form nor beauty-yet He is the chosen Servant of God
4) He is rejected and despised by men but He is the appointed Savior
5) He suffers until death but survives
6) He has no offspring but He has a numerous seed
7) They made His grave with the wicked but He is buried with the rich
8) He suffers greatly but prospers
9) He is triumphed over yet He is victorious
10) He is condemned yet He justifies the condemned
11) Men thought He was stricken by God yet "He shall be exalted and extolled and be very high."

These apparent contradictions were DESIGNED to be a prophetic puzzle and they remained a problem until Jesus died on the cross, was buried in the rich mans tomb, was resurrected and went up to reign in triumph in Heaven. [Paraphrased from MESSIAH IN BOTH TESTAMENTS page 63 which was quoting from LIVING ORACLES, page 110.]

THE SUFFERING SERVANT
Isaiah prophesized more than 700 years before the Messiah, Jesus the Christ, came.

THE HUMILIATION
He will be widely rejected.
FORETOLD

Isaiah 53;1,3 "Who has believed our report? And to whom has the arm of the LORD been revealed? . . . He is despised and rejected by men, a Man of sorrows and acquainted with grief. And we hid, as it were, our faces from Him; He was despised, and we did not esteem Him."

FULFILLED

John 12:37-38 "But although He had done so many signs before them, they did not believe in Him, that the word of Isaiah the prophet might be fulfilled, which he spoke: 'Lord, who has believed our report? And to whom has the arm of the LORD been revealed?'" See also John 11:45-57; Matthew 26:1-5; Mark 14:1-2; Luke 22:1-2.

He will be disfigured by suffering.
FORETOLD

Isaiah 50:5-6 "The Lord GOD has opened My ear; and I was not rebellious, nor did I turn away. I gave My back to those who struck Me, and My cheeks to those who plucked out the beard; I did not hide my face from shame and spitting."

Isaiah 52:14 "Just as many were astonished at you, so His visage was marred more than any man, and His form more than the sons of men;"

Isaiah 53:2 "For He shall grow up before Him as a tender plant, and as a root out of dry ground. He has no form of comeliness; and when we see Him, there is no beauty that we should desire Him."

FULFILLED

Matthew 27:26-31 "Then he released Barabbas to them; and when he had scourged Jesus, he delivered Him to be crucified. Then the soldiers of the governor took Jesus into the Praetorium and gathered the whole garrison around Him. And they stripped Him and put a scarlet robe on Him. When they had twisted a crown of thorns, they put it on His head, and a reed in His right hand. And they bowed the knee before Him and mocked Him, saying, 'Hail, King of the Jews!' Then they spat on Him, and took the reed and struck Him on the head. And when they had mocked Him, they took the robe off Him, put His own clothes on Him, and led Him away to be crucified." See also Mark 15:6-20; Luke 23:13-24 and John 18:39-19:16.

He will bear our sins and sorrows and make a blood atonement.
FORETOLD

Isaiah 53:4-5 "Surely He has borne our griefs and carried our sorrows; yet we esteemed Him stricken, smitten by God, and afflicted. But He was wounded for our transgressions, He was bruised for our iniquities; the chastisement for our peace was upon Him, and by His stripes we are healed."

FULFILLED

1 Peter 2:24-25 "who Himself bore our sins in His own body on the tree, that we, having died to sins, might live for righteousness—by whose stripes you were healed. For you were like sheep going astray, but have now returned to the Shepherd and Overseer of your souls."

Romans 3:25-26 "whom God set forth as a propitiation by His blood, through faith, to demonstrate His righteousness, because in His forbearance God had passed over the sins that were previously committed, to demonstrate at the present time His righteousness, that He might be just and the justifier of the one who has faith in Jesus."

Romans 4:25 Jesus: "who was delivered up because of our offenses, and was raised because of our justification."

1 John 4:10 "In this is love, not that we loved God, but that He loved us and sent His Son to be the propitiation *[atonement]* for our sins." *Italics added for clarity.*

He will be our substitute and voluntarily accept our guilt and punishment.
FORETOLD

Isaiah 53:6-8 "All we like sheep have gone astray; we have turned every one, to his own way; and the LORD has laid on Him the iniquity of us all. He was oppressed and He was afflicted, yet He opened not His mouth; He was led as a lamb to the slaughter, and as a sheep before its shearers is silent, so He opened not His mouth. He was taken from prison and from judgment, and who will declare His generation? For He was cut off from the land of the living; for the transgressions of My people He was stricken."

FULFILLED

2 Corinthians 5:21 "For He made Him who knew no sin to be sin for us, that we might become the righteousness of God in Him." See also Romans 1:17; 3:21-24.

Matthew 27:12-14 "And while He was being accused by the chief priests and elders, He answered nothing. Then Pilate said to Him, 'Do You not hear how many things they testify against You?' but He answered him not one word, so that the governor marveled greatly." See also Mark 15:2-5; Luke 23:2-5; John 18:29-38.

He will die with transgressors and be buried in a rich man's tomb.
FORETOLD

Isaiah 53:9, 12 "And they made His grave with the wicked-but with the rich at His death, because He had done no violence, nor was any deceit in His mouth . . . Therefore I will divide Him a portion with the great, and He shall divide the spoil with the strong, because He poured out His soul unto death, and He was numbered with the transgressors, and He bore the sin of many, and made intercession for the transgressors."

FULFILLED

Luke 23:32-34a, "There were also two others, criminals, led with Him to be put to death. And when they had come to the place called Calvary, there they crucified Him, and the criminals, one on the right hand and the other on the left. Then Jesus said, 'Father, forgive them, for they do not know what they do.'"

50-53 "Now behold, there was a man named Joseph, a council member, a good and just man. He had not consented to their decision and deed. He was from Arimathea, a city of the Jews, who himself was also waiting for the kingdom of God. This man went to Pilate and asked for the body of Jesus. Then he took it down, wrapped it in linen, and laid it in a tomb that was hewn out of the rock, where no one had ever lain before." See also Matthew 27:38, 57-60; Mark 15:27-28, 42-46; John 19:18, 38-42.

He will justify many from their sins.
FORETOLD

Isaiah 53:10-11 "Yet it pleased the LORD to bruise Him; He has put Him to grief. When You make His soul an offering for sin, He shall see His seed, He shall prolong His days, and the pleasure of the LORD shall prosper in His hand. He shall see the labor of His soul, and be satisfied. By His knowledge My righteous Servant shall justify many, for He shall bear their iniquities."

FULFILLED

Romans 5:18-19 "Therefore, as through one man's offense judgment came to all men, resulting in condemnation, even so through one Man's righteous act the free gift came to all men, resulting in justification of life. For as by one man's disobedience many were made sinners, so also by one Man's obedience many will be made righteous," See also Romans 5:12-17.

Matthew 26:39-42 "He went a little farther and fell on His face, and prayed, saying, 'O My Father, if it is possible, let this cup pass from Me; nevertheless, not as I will, but as You will.' Then He came to the disciples and found them sleeping, and said to Peter, 'What! Could you not watch with Me one hour? Watch and pray, lest you enter into temptation. The spirit indeed is willing, but the flesh is weak.' Again, a second time, He went away and prayed, saying, 'O My Father, if this cup cannot pass away from Me unless I drink it, Your will be done.'" See also Mark 14:32-42; Luke 22:39-46.

Hebrews 10:4-7,10 "For it is not possible that the blood of bulls and goats could take away sins. Therefore, when He came into the world, He said: 'Sacrifice and offering You did not desire, but a body You have prepared for Me. In burnt offerings and sacrifices for sin You had no pleasure. Then I said, "Behold, I have come—in the volume of the book it is written of Me—to do Your will, O God." [Psalm 40:6-8] ...By that will we have been sanctified *[set apart]* through the offering of the body of Jesus Christ once for all." *[Italic added for clarity]* See also Mark 12:28-34.

THE EXALTATION
He will be exalted.
FORETOLD

Isaiah 52:13 "Behold, My Servant shall deal prudently; He shall be exalted and extolled and be very high."

Isaiah 53:10b-12a "He shall see His seed, He shall prolong His days, and the pleasure of the LORD shall prosper in His hand. He shall see the labor of His soul, and be satisfied. By His knowledge My righteous Servant shall justify many, for He shall bear their iniquities. Therefore I will divide Him a portion with the great, and He shall divide the spoil with the strong.

FULFILLED

Philippians 2:9-11 "Therefore God also has highly exalted Him and given Him the name which is above every name, that at the name of Jesus every knee should bow, of those in heaven, and of those on earth, and of those under the earth, and that every tongue should confess that Jesus Christ is Lord, to the glory of God the Father." See also verses 5-8.

Matthew 28:18-20 "And Jesus came and spoke to them, saying, 'All authority has been given to Me in heaven and on earth. Go therefore and make disciples of all the nations, baptizing them in the name of the Father and of the Son and of the Holy Spirit, teaching them to observe all things that I have commanded you; and lo, I am with you always, even to the end of the age.' Amen."

Luke 24:44-53 "Then He said to them, 'These are the words which I spoke to you while I was still with you, that all things must be fulfilled which were written in the Law of Moses and the Prophets and the Psalms concerning Me.' And He opened their understanding, that they might comprehend the Scriptures.

Then He said to them, 'Thus it is written, and thus it was necessary for the Christ to suffer and to rise from the dead the third day, and that repentance and remission of sins should be preached in His name to all nations, beginning at Jerusalem. And you are witnesses of these things. Behold, I send the Promise of My Father upon you; but tarry in the city of Jerusalem until you are endued with power from on high.'

And He led them out as far as Bethany, and He lifted up His hands and blessed them. Now it came to pass, while He blessed them, that He was parted from them and carried up into heaven. And they worshiped Him and returned to Jerusalem with great joy, and were continually in the temple praising and blessing God. Amen."

NO BONES BROKEN
FORETOLD

A Psalm of King David.
Psalm 34:20 "He guards all his bones; not one of them is broken."

Zechariah means Yahweh Remembers, he wrote between 520-518B.C.

Zechariah 12:10 "And I will pour on the house of David and on the inhabitants of Jerusalem the Spirit of grace and supplication; then they will look on Me whom they pierced. Yes, they will mourn for Him as one mourns for his only son, and grieve for Him as one grieves for a firstborn."

FULFILLED

John 19:31-37 "Therefore, because it was the Preparation Day, that the bodies should not remain on the cross on the Sabbath (for that Sabbath was a high day), the Jews asked Pilate that their legs might be broken, and that they might be taken away. Then the soldiers came and broke the legs of the first and of the other who was crucified with Him. But when they came to Jesus and saw that He was already dead, they did not break His legs. But one of the soldiers pierced His side with a spear, and immediately blood and water came out, and he who has seen has testified, and his testimony is true; and he knows that he is telling the truth, so that you may believe. For these things were done that the Scripture should be fulfilled. 'Not one of His bones shall be broken.' And again another Scripture says, 'They shall look on Him whom they pierced.'"

CHAPTER 7: THE CRUCIFIXION

PSALM 22

Please read all of Psalm 22. King David wrote this Psalm 1000 years before it was fulfilled by Jesus on the cross. The miracle of this Psalm is that the Jews did not know about crucifixion, they punished criminals by stoning. Crucifixion was a Roman punishment and the nation of Rome did not exist until several centuries later. Constantine the Great stopped the punishment of crucifixion in 337AD out of respect for Jesus Christ. Psalm 22 vividly pictures:

THE SUFFERINGS OF THE MESSIAH
1) Forsaken by God, crying out day and night [versus 1-5];
2) Reproached, despised and ridiculed by men [versus 6-8];
3) Yet He was righteous He had trusted in God from birth [versus 9-10];
4) He is left with no one to help and surrounded by His enemies [versus 11-13,16];
5) His hands and feet are pierced, His entire body is in agony until relieved by death [versus 14-15,16b-17a];
6) They stare at Him, divide His garments and cast lots for His clothing [versus 17b-18];
7) **BUT HIS ONLY HOPE IS IN GOD** [versus 19-21a];
GOD RESCUES HIM [versus 21b]
8) Verse 22 begins a new section as the Messiah, now delivered through resurrection, praises God for His faithfulness.
9) All shall praise and worship the LORD to the ends of the world [versus 23-27];
10) Because He rules over the nations [verse 28];
11) Even those that have died and those yet to be born shall declare His righteousness [versus 29-31].

Condensed and paraphrased from MESSIAH IN BOTH TESTAMENTS, pages 59-63 by Fred John Meldau. [Can be downloaded from the Internet]

PSALM 22: THE SUFFERING OF THE MESSIAH FORETOLD

A Psalm of King David.
David reigned between 1010-970B.C.

Verse 1-2 "**My God, My God, why have You forsaken Me?** Why are You so far from helping Me, and from the words of My groaning? O My God, I cry in the daytime, but You do not hear; and in the night season, and am not silent." [bold added]

Amos 8:9 "'And it shall come to pass in that day', says the Lord GOD, 'that I will make the sun go down at noon, and I will darken the earth in broad daylight;'"

Verses 6-8 "But I am a worm, and no man; a reproach of men, and despised by the people. All those who see Me ridicule Me; they shoot out the lip, they shake the head. saying, He trusted in the Lord, let Him rescue Him; let Him deliver Him, since He delights in Him!"

Verses 14-18 "I am poured out like water, and all My bones are out of joint; My heart is like wax; it has melted within Me. My strength is dried up like a potsherd, and My tongue clings to My jaws; You have brought Me to the dust of death. For dogs have surrounded Me; the congregation of the wicked has enclosed Me. They pierced My hands and My feet; I can count all My bones. They look and stare at Me. They divide My garments among them, and for My clothing they cast lots."

FULFILLED

Matthew 27:35-46 "Then they crucified Him, and divided His garments, casting lots, that it might be fulfilled which was spoken by the prophet:

'They divided My garments among them, and for My clothing they cast lots.' Sitting down, they kept watch over Him there. And they put up over His head the accusation written against Him: THIS IS JESUS THE KING OF THE JEWS. Then two robbers were crucified with Him, one on the right and another on the left.

And those who passed by blasphemed Him, wagging their heads and saying, "You who destroy the temple and build it in three days, save Yourself! If You are the Son of God, come down from the cross.'

Likewise the chief priests also, mocking with the scribes and elders, said, 'He saved others; Himself He cannot save. If He is the King of Israel, let Him now come down from the cross, and we will believe Him. He trusted in God; let Him deliver Him now if He will have Him; for He said, "I am the Son of God."

Even the robbers who were crucified with Him reviled Him with the same thing.

Now from the sixth hour until the ninth hour there was darkness over all the land. And about the ninth hour Jesus cried out with a loud voice, saying, 'Eli, Eli, lama sabachthani? that is, **My God, My God, why have You forsaken Me?**'" See also Mark 15:21-41; Luke 23:26-49; John 19:17-30.

"**27:45 The sixth hour** was noon. The **darkness** was not due to an eclipse of the sun, since the Passover occurred at full moon. This was a supernatural occurrence." The NELSON STUDY BIBLE page 1632

FROM MY MOTHERS WOMB YOU HAVE BEEN MY GOD
FORETOLD

Psalm 22:9-10 "But You are He who took Me Out of the womb; You made Me trust while on My mother's breasts. I was cast upon You from birth. From My mother's womb You have been My God."

FULFILLED

Luke 1:26-38 "Now in the sixth month the angel Gabriel was sent by God to a city of Galilee named Nazareth, to a virgin betrothed to a man whose name was Joseph, of the house of David. The virgin's name was Mary. And having come in, the angel said to her, 'Rejoice, highly favored one, the Lord is with you; blessed are you among women!'

But when she saw him, she was troubled at his saying, and considered what manner of greeting this was. Then the angel said to her, 'Do not be afraid, Mary, for you have found favor with God. And behold, you will conceive in your womb and bring forth a Son, and shall call His name JESUS. He will be great, and will be called the Son of the Highest; and the Lord God will give Him the throne of His father David. And He will reign over the house of Jacob forever, and of His kingdom there will be no end.'

Then Mary said to the angel, 'How can this be, since I do not know a man?'

And the angel answered and said to her, 'The Holy Spirit will come upon you, and the power of the Highest will overshadow you; therefore, also, that Holy One who is to be born will be called the Son of God. Now indeed, Elizabeth your relative has also conceived a son in her old age; and this is now the sixth month for her who was called barren. For with God nothing will be impossible.'

Then Mary said, 'Behold the maidservant of the Lord! Let it be to me according to your word.' And the angel departed from her." See also Matthew 1:18-25.

Read all of Luke chapters 1 and 2 and pay close attention to what Elizabeth says to Mary while filled with the Holy Spirit. Luke 1:41b-45 "and Elizabeth was filled with the Holy Spirit. Then she spoke out with a loud voice and said, 'Blessed are you among women, and blessed is the fruit of your womb! But why is this granted to me, that the mother of my Lord should come to me? For indeed, as soon as the voice of your greeting sounded in my ears, the babe leaped in my womb for joy. Blessed is she who believed, for there will be a fulfillment of those things which were told her from the Lord." And Simeon, while the Holy Spirit was upon him, said in verses 30-32 of chapter 2: "For my eyes have seen Your salvation which You have prepared before the face of all peoples, a light to bring revelation to the Gentiles, and the glory of Your people Israel."

HIS ONLY HOPE IS IN GOD
FORETOLD

GOD HAS ALREADY PROVED THAT HE CAN BE TRUSTED

Psalm 22:3-5 "But You are holy, enthroned in the praises of Israel. Our fathers trusted in You; they trusted, and You delivered them. They cried to You, and were delivered; they trusted in You, and were not ashamed.

HIS ONLY HOPE IS IN GOD

Psalm 22:19-21 "But You, O LORD, do not be far from Me; O My Strength, hasten to help Me! Deliver Me from the sword, My precious life from the power of the dog. Save Me from the lion's mouth and from the horns of the wild oxen! You have answered Me."

Psalm 31:5 "Into Your hand I commit my spirit; You have redeemed me, O LORD God of truth."

FULFILLED

Luke 23:46-47 "And when Jesus had cried out with a loud voice, He said, 'Father, into Your hands I commit My spirit.' Having said this, He breathed His last.

So when the centurion saw what had happened, he glorified God, saying, 'Certainly this was a righteous Man!'"

He is risen! Luke 24:1-9 "Now on the first day of the week, very early in the morning, they, and certain other women with them, came to the tomb bringing the spices which they had prepared. But they found the stone rolled away from the tomb. Then they went in and did not find the body of the Lord Jesus. And it happened as they were greatly perplexed about this, that behold, two men stood by them in shining garments. Then, as they were afraid and bowed their faces to the earth, they said to them, 'Why do you seek the living among the dead? He is not here, but is risen! Remember how He spoke to you when He was still in Galilee, saying, "The Son of Man must be delivered into the hands of sinful men, and be crucified, and the third day rise again."'

And they remembered His words. Then they returned from the tomb and told all these things to the eleven and to all the rest." See also Matthew 27:45-28:10; Mark 15:33-16:8; John 19:25-20:10.

THE JOYFUL CELEBRATION OF GREAT VICTORY FORETOLD

I WILL DECLARE YOUR NAME TO MY BRETHREN

Psalm 22:22-26 "I will declare Your name to My brethren; in the midst of the assembly I will praise You. You who fear the LORD, praise Him! All you descendants of Jacob, glorify Him, and fear Him, all you offspring of Israel! For He has not despised nor abhorred the affliction of the afflicted; nor has He hidden His face from Him; but when He cried to Him, He heard. My praise shall be of You in the great assembly; I will pay My vows before those who fear Him. The poor shall eat and be satisfied; those who seek Him will praise the LORD. Let your heart live forever!"

TO THE END OF THE WORLD ALL SHALL WORSHIP BEFORE YOU

Psalm 22:27-28 "All the ends of the world shall remember and turn to the LORD, and all the families of the nations shall worship before You. For the kingdom is the LORD'S, and He rules over the nations."

THOSE THAT HAVE DIED, THOSE THAT ARE ALIVE, AND THOSE YET TO BE BORN WILL WORSHIP HIM AND DECLARE HIS RIGHTEOUSNESS

Psalm 22:29-31 "All the prosperous of the earth shall eat and worship; all those who go down to the dust shall bow before Him, even he who cannot keep himself alive. A posterity shall serve Him. It will be recounted of the Lord to the next generation, they will come and declare His righteousness to a people who will be born, that He has done this."

FULFILLED

Hebrews 2:10-12 "For it was fitting for Him, for whom are all things and by whom are all things, in bringing many sons to glory, to make the captain of their salvation perfect through sufferings. For both He who sanctifies and those who are being sanctified are all of one, for which reason He is not ashamed to call them brethren, saying:
'I will declare Your name to My brethren; in the midst of the assembly I will sing praise to You."
Romans 8:28-29 "And we know that all things work together for good to those who love God, to those who are the called according to His purpose. For whom He foreknew, He also predestined to be conformed to the image of His Son, that He might be the firstborn among many brethren."
Matthew 6:10 "Your kingdom come. Your will be done on earth as it is in heaven."
Verse 13b "For Yours is the kingdom and the power and the glory forever. Amen."

CHAPTER 8: THE RESURECTION

THE RESURECTION
FORETOLD
A Psalm of King David.

Psalm 16:10 "For You will not leave my soul in Sheol *(the grave)*, nor will You allow Your Holy One to see corruption." *(Italics added for clarity)*

A Psalm of the sons of Korah. See Numbers 16:1-35, pay close attention to verse 27. Then read Numbers 26:9-11 and notice that the family of Korah did not stand with him against Moses.

Psalm 49:15 "But God will redeem my soul from the power of the grave, for He shall receive me."

FULFILLED

Mark 16:1-14 "Now when the Sabbath was past, Mary Magdalene, Mary the mother of James, and Salome bought spices, that they might come and anoint Him. Very early in the morning, on the first day of the week, they came to the tomb when the sun had risen. And they said among themselves, 'Who will roll away the stone from the door of the tomb for us?' But when they looked up, they saw that the stone had been rolled away—for it was very large. And entering the tomb, they saw a young man clothed in a long white robe sitting on the right side; and they were alarmed.

But he said to them, 'Do not be alarmed. You seek Jesus of Nazareth, who was crucified. He is risen! He is not here. See the place where they laid Him. But go, tell His disciples--and Peter—that He is going before you into Galilee; there you will see Him, as He said to you.'

So they went out quickly and fled from the tomb, for they trembled and were amazed. And they said nothing to anyone, for they were afraid.

Now when He rose early on the first day of the week, He appeared first to Mary Magdalene, out of whom He had cast seven demons. She went and told those who had been with Him, as they mourned and wept. And when they heard that He was alive and had been seen by her, they did not believe.

After that, He appeared in another form to two of them as they walked and went into the country. And they went and told it to the rest, but they did not believe them either.

Later He appeared to the eleven as they sat at the table; and He rebuked their unbelief and hardness of heart, because they did not believe those who had seen Him after He had risen." See also Matthew 28:1-20; Luke 24:1-49; John 20:1-31.

ASCENDED TO GOD'S RIGHT HAND
FORETOLD
Psalms of David

Psalm 110:1-2 "The LORD said to my Lord, 'Sit at My right hand, till I make Your enemies Your footstool.' The LORD shall send the rod of Your strength out of Zion. Rule in the midst of Your enemies!"

Psalm 68:18 "You have ascended on high, You have led captivity captive; You have received gifts among men, even from the rebellious, that the LORD God might dwell there."

FULFILLED

Matthew 22:41-45 "While the Pharisees were gathered together, Jesus asked them, saying, 'What do you think about the Christ? Whose Son is He?'

They said to Him, 'The Son of David.'

He said to them, 'How then does David in the Spirit call Him "Lord," saying:

"The LORD said to my Lord, 'Sit at My right hand, till I make Your enemies Your footstool"?

If David then calls Him 'Lord,' how is He his Son?"

See also Mark 12:35-37; Luke 20:41-44.

Luke 24:50-52 "And He led them out as far as Bethany, and He lifted up His hands and blessed them. Now it came to pass, while He blessed them, that He was parted from them and carried up into heaven. And they worshiped Him, and returned to Jerusalem with great joy." See also Mark 16:19-20; Acts 1:9; 7:55-56; Ephesians 1:20; Hebrews 1:3

Ephesians 4:7-8 "But to each one of us grace was given according to the measure of Christ's gift. Therefore He says:

'When He ascended on high, He led captivity captive, and gave gifts to men.'

See also Romans 12:3-8; Acts 10:44-48; 11:16-17.

WHAT THE RESURECTION OF JESUS CHRIST MEANS TO US AND FOR US

ALL the promises of God in Him are YES!

2Corinthians 1:19-20 "For the Son of God, Jesus Christ, who was preached among you by us—by me, Silvanus, and Timothy—was not Yes and No, but in Him was Yes. For all the promises of God in Him are Yes, and in Him Amen, to the glory of God through us."

He does not change!

Hebrews 13:8 "Jesus Christ is the same yesterday, today, and forever."

ALL people, Jews and Gentiles, share in the PROMISES of God!

Romans 15:8-13 "Now I say that Jesus Christ has become a servant to the circumcision for the truth of God, to confirm the promises made to the fathers, and that the Gentiles might glorify God for His mercy, as it is written:
  'For this reason I will confess to You among the Gentiles, and sing to Your
  name.' [2 Samuel 22:50; Psalm 18:49]
And again he says:
  'Rejoice, O Gentiles, with His people!' [Deuteronomy 32:43]
And again:
  'Praise the LORD, all you Gentiles!
  Laud Him, all you peoples!' [Psalms 117:1]
And again, Isaiah says:
  'There shall be a root of Jesse;
  And He who shall rise to reign over the Gentiles,
  In Him the Gentiles shall hope.' [Isaiah 11:10]
  Now may the God of hope fill you with all joy and peace in believing, that you may abound in hope by the power of the Holy Spirit."

He secured our resurrection!

Romans 4:24-25 "but also for us. It shall be imputed to us who believe in Him who raised up Jesus our Lord from the dead, who was delivered up because of our offenses, and was raised because of our justification." See also verses 13-23.
  "**4:25** Jesus was **delivered up** to death, taking the penalty of our sin on Himself. Just as God brought life from Abraham and Sarah, who thought they were unable to have children, so God **raised** Jesus back to life. Jesus' resurrection brought us justification before God because the Resurrection proves that God accepted Jesus' sacrifice for us." The NELSON STUDY BIBLE page 1886

  Romans 8:11 "But if the Spirit of Him who raised Jesus from the dead dwells in you, He who raised Christ from the dead will also give life to your mortal bodies through His Spirit who dwells in you."
  See also 1 Corinthians 6:14; 15:47-49; Philippians 3:21; 1 John 3:1-3.

CHAPTER 9: THE FREE GIFT

THE UNIQUENESS OF CHRISTIANITY

"Judaism sees salvation as a judgment day decision based on morality. Hindus anticipate multiple reincarnations in the soul's journey through the cosmos. Buddhism guides your life according to the Four Noble Truths and the Noble Eight-fold Path. Muslims earn their way to Allah through the Five Pillars of Faith. Many philosophers deem life after death as hidden and unknown, 'a great leap in the dark.' Some people clump Christ with Moses, Mohammad, Confucius, and other spiritual leaders. But Jesus declares, 'I am the way, and the truth, and the life. No one comes to the Father except through me.' Many object, 'All roads lead to heaven.' But how can they? Buddhists look toward Nirvana, achieved after no less than 547 reincarnations. Christians believe in one life, one death, and an eternity of enjoying God. Humanists don't acknowledge a creator of life. Jesus claims to be the source of life. Spiritualists read your palms. Christians consult the Bible. Hindus perceive a plural and impersonal God. Christ-followers believe 'there is only one God' (1 Cor. 8:4 NLT). Every non-Christian religion says, 'You can save you.' Jesus says: 'My death on the cross saves you.' All roads don't lead to London, all ships don't sail to Australia, and all flights don't land in Rome. Every path does not lead to God. Jesus blazed a stand-alone trail void of self-salvation. He cleared a one-of-a-kind passageway uncluttered by human effort. He offers us a unique invitation in which He works and we trust, He dies and we live, He invites and we believe. 'The work God wants you to do is this: Believe the One he sent' (Jn 6:29 NCV)." Taken from the WORD FOR YOU TODAY, Monday October 26, 2009.

IN THE WORDS OF JESUS

PLEASE READ ALL OF JOHN 6. John 6:28-29 "Then they said to Him, 'What shall we do, that we may work the works of God?' Jesus answered and said to them, 'This is the work of God, that you believe in Him whom He sent.'"

37-40 "All that the Father gives Me will come to Me, and the one who comes to Me I will by no means cast out. For I have come down from heaven, not to do My own will, but the will of Him who sent Me. This is the will of the Father who sent Me, that of all He has given Me I should lose nothing, but should raise it up at the last day. And this is the will of Him who sent Me, that everyone who sees the Son and believes in Him may have everlasting life; and I will raise him up at the last day."

44-45 "No one can come to Me unless the Father who sent Me draws him; and I will raise him up at the last day. It is written in the prophets, 'And they shall all be taught by God' *(Isaiah 54:13)*. Therefore everyone who has heard and learned from the Father comes to Me." *Italics added.*

47-48 "Most assuredly, I say to you, he who believes in Me has everlasting life. I am the bread of life."

51 "I am the living bread which came down from heaven. If anyone eats of this bread, he will live forever; and the bread that I shall give is My flesh, which I shall give for the life of the world." **Eats of this bread** is a synonym for faith. 35 "And Jesus said to them, 'I am the bread of life. He who comes to Me shall never hunger, and he who believes in Me shall never thirst." 48-50 "I am the bread of life. Your fathers ate the manna in the wilderness, and are dead. This is the bread which comes down from heaven, that one may eat of it and not die."

It was His death on the cross that gave us the gift of eternal life. Like any gift it must be received and accepted to be ours. If we reject the free gift of eternal life we will die in our sins. It is faith in the sacrifice of Jesus the Christ that gives us life. "For God so loved the world that He gave His only begotten Son, that whoever believes in Him should not perish but have everlasting life. For God did not send His Son into the world to condemn the world, but that the world through Him might be saved. He who believes in Him is not condemned; but he who does not believe is condemned already, because he has not believed in the name of the only begotten Son of God." John 3:16-18

HOW TO RECEIVE AND ACCEPT THE FREE GIFT OF GOD

1) CONFESS OUR SINS

Romans 6:23 "For the wages of sin is death, but the <u>gift of God</u> is eternal life in Christ Jesus our Lord."

1 John 1:8-9 "If we say that we have no sin, we deceive ourselves, and the truth is not in us. If we confess our sins, He is faithful and just to forgive us our sins and to cleanse us from all unrighteousness."

2) BELIEVE IN THE LORD JESUS

Romans 10:9-10 "that if you confess with your mouth the Lord Jesus and believe in your heart that God has raised Him from the dead, you will be saved. For with the heart one believes unto righteousness, and with the mouth confession is made unto salvation."

Ephesians 2:8-9 "For by grace you have been saved through faith, and that not of yourselves; it is the <u>gift of God</u> not of works, lest anyone should boast."

Acts 4:12 "Nor is there salvation in any other, for there is no other name under heaven given among men by which we must be saved." *[Peter speaking of Jesus under the influence of the Holy Spirit. Acts 4:8-12]*

3) LIVE BY FAITH

Romans 1:16-17 "For I am not ashamed of the gospel *[good news]* of Christ, for it is the power of God to salvation for everyone who believes, for the Jew first and also for the Greek. For in it the righteousness of God is revealed from <u>faith to faith</u> as it is written, 'The just shall live by faith.'" *[Habakkuk 2:4] Underlining and italics added for emphasis.*

"If you'd like to begin a personal relationship with Jesus today, please pray this prayer:
Lord Jesus, I invite you into my life. I believe You died for me and that Your blood pays for my sins and provides me with the gift of eternal life. By faith I receive that gift, and I acknowledge You as my Lord and Savior. Amen." [from THE WORD FOR YOU TODAY page 53]

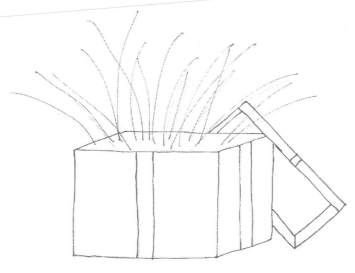

CHAPTER 10: THE PROMISED KINGDOM

JESUS IS THE KING IN THE KINGDOM OF GOD FORETOLD

Daniel was taken captive by King Nebuchadnezzar in 605BC and interprets the Kings' dream in 603BC. The dream is in Daniel chapter 2.

Daniel 2:44 "And in the days of these kings the God of heaven will set up a kingdom which shall never be destroyed; and the kingdom shall not be left to other people; it shall break in pieces and consume all these kingdoms, and it shall stand forever." See also Isaiah 9:6-7; 7:14; 60:12; 2 Samuel 7:12-17; Psalm 89:34-37 and please read all of Daniel chapter 2.

THE ANGEL GABRIEL TALKS TO MARY

Luke 1:31-33 "And behold, you will conceive in your womb and bring forth a Son, and shall call His name JESUS. He will be great, and will be called the Son of the Highest; and the Lord God will give Him the throne of His father David. And He will reign over the house of Jacob forever, and of His kingdom there will be no end."

JESUS RULES IN THE MIIDST OF HIS ENEMIES
FORETOLD

Psalm 110:1-2 "The LORD said to my Lord, 'Sit at My right hand, till I make Your enemies Your footstool.'

The LORD shall send the rod of Your strength out of Zion. Rule in the midst of Your enemies!"

Isaiah 66:1a "Thus says the LORD: 'Heaven is My throne, and earth is My footstool.'"

Psalm 2:1-12 "Why do the nations rage, and the people plot a vain thing? The kings of the earth set themselves, and the rulers take counsel together, against the LORD and against His Anointed, saying, 'Let us break Their bonds in pieces and cast away Their cords from us'

He who sits in the heavens shall laugh; the LORD shall hold them in derision. Then He shall speak to them in His wrath, and distress them in His deep displeasure:

'Yet I have set My King on My holy hill of Zion.'

'I will declare the decree: the LORD has said to Me, "You are My Son, today I have begotten You. Ask of Me, and I will give You the nations for Your inheritance, and the ends of the earth for Your possession. You shall break them with a rod of iron; You shall dash them to pieces like a potter's vessel."

Now therefore, be wise, O kings; be instructed, you judges of the earth. Serve the LORD with fear, and rejoice with trembling. Kiss the Son, lest He be angry, and you perish in the way, when His wrath is kindled but a little. Blessed are all those who put their trust in Him."

FULFILLED

Luke 10:17-20 "Then the seventy returned with joy, saying, 'Lord, even the demons are subject to us in Your name.'

And He said to them, 'I saw Satan fall like lightning from heaven. Behold, I give you the authority to trample on serpents and scorpions, and over all the power of the enemy, and nothing shall by any means hurt you. Nevertheless do not rejoice in this, that the spirits are subject to you, but rather rejoice because your names are written in heaven.'"

Revelation 12:7-12 "And war broke out in heaven; Michael and his angels fought with the dragon; and the dragon and his angels fought, but they did not prevail, nor was a place found for them in heaven any longer. So the great dragon was cast out, that serpent of old, called the Devil and Satan, who deceives the whole world; he was cast to the earth, and his angels were cast out with him.

Then I heard a loud voice saying in heaven, 'Now salvation, and strength, and the kingdom of our God, and the power of His Christ have come, for the accuser of our brethren, who accused them before our God day and night, has been cast down. And they overcame him by the blood of the Lamb and by the word of their testimony, and they did not love their lives to the death. Therefore rejoice, O heavens, and you who dwell in them! Woe to the inhabitants of the earth and the sea! For the devil has come down to you, having great wrath, because he knows that he has a short time.'"

THE KING IS GIVEN HIS EVERLASTING KINGDOM
FORETOLD

Daniel 7:13-14 "I was watching in the night visions, and behold, One like the Son of Man, coming with the clouds of heaven! He came to the Ancient of Days, and they brought Him near before Him. Then to Him was given dominion and glory and a kingdom, that all peoples, nations, and languages should serve Him. His dominion is an everlasting dominion, which shall not pass away, and His kingdom *the one* which shall not be destroyed."

FULFILLED

Matthew 28:18-19 "And Jesus came and spoke to them, saying, 'All authority has been given to Me in heaven and on earth. Go therefore and make disciples of all the nations, baptizing them in the name of the Father and of the Son and of the Holy Spirit, teaching them to observe all things that I have commanded you; and lo, I am with you always, even to the end of the age.' Amen." See also Mark 16:14-20.

Acts 1:8-11 "But you shall receive power when the Holy Spirit has come upon you; and you shall be witnesses to Me in Jerusalem, and in all Judea and Samaria, and to the end of the earth.'

Now when He had spoken these things, while they watched, He was taken up, and a cloud received Him out of their sight. And while they looked steadfastly toward heaven as He went up, behold, two men stood by them in white apparel, who also said, 'Men of Galilee, why do you stand gazing up into heaven? This *same* Jesus, who was taken up from you into heaven, will so come in like manner as you saw Him go into heaven.'"

THE PROMISED KINGDOM

2 Corinthians 1:20 "For all the promises of God in Him are Yes, and in Him Amen *[so be it]*, to the glory of God through us." *[Italics added for clarity]*.

Isaiah 11:1-10 "There shall come forth a Rod *[Jesus]* from the stem of Jesse *[Jesse was the father of King David]*, and a Branch shall grow out of his roots. The Spirit of the LORD shall rest upon Him, the Spirit of wisdom and understanding, the Spirit of counsel and might, the Spirit of knowledge and of the fear of the LORD. His delight is in the fear of the LORD, and He shall not judge by the sight of His eyes, nor decide by the hearing of His ears; but with righteousness He shall judge the poor, and decide with equity for the meek of the earth; He shall strike the earth with the rod of His mouth, and with the breath of His lips He shall slay the wicked. Righteousness shall be the belt of His loins, and faithfulness the belt of His waist.

The wolf also shall dwell with the lamb, the leopard shall lie down with the young goat, the calf and the young lion and the fatling together; and a little child shall lead them. The cow and the bear shall graze; their young ones shall lie down together; and the lion shall eat straw like the ox. The nursing child shall play by the cobra's hole, and the weaned child shall put his hand in the viper's den. They shall not hurt nor destroy in all My holy mountain, for the earth shall be full of the knowledge of the LORD as the waters cover the sea.

And in that day there shall be a Root of Jesse, who shall stand as a banner to the people; for <u>the Gentiles shall seek Him, and His resting place shall be glorious.</u>"

Isaiah 65:17-25 "For behold, I create **new heavens and a new earth**; and the former shall not be remembered or come to mind. But be glad and rejoice forever in what I create; for behold, I create Jerusalem as a rejoicing, and her people a joy. I will rejoice in Jerusalem, and joy in My people; the voice of weeping shall no longer be heard in her, nor the voice of crying.

No more shall an infant from there live but a few days, nor an old man who has not fulfilled his days; for the child shall die one hundred years old, but the sinner being one hundred years old shall be accursed.

They shall build houses and inhabit them; they shall plant vineyards and eat their fruit. They shall not build and another inhabit; they shall not plant and another eat; for as the days of a tree, so shall be the days of My people, and My elect shall long enjoy the work of their hands. They shall not labor in vain, nor bring forth children for trouble; for they shall be the descendants of the blessed of the LORD, and their offspring with them.

It shall come to pass that before they call, I will answer; and while they are still speaking. I will hear.

The wolf and the lamb shall feed together, the lion shall eat straw like the ox, and dust shall be the serpent's food. They shall not hurt nor destroy in all My holy mountain,' says the LORD." See also Isaiah 66:22-23.

Isaiah 2:4 "He shall judge between the nations, and rebuke many people; they shall beat their swords into plowshares, and their spears into pruning hooks; nation shall not lift up sword against nation, neither shall they learn war anymore." Read also verses 2-3 and Micah 4:1-5.

Isaiah 9:6-7 "For unto us a Child is born, unto us a Son is given; and the government will he upon His shoulder. And His name will be called Wonderful, Counselor, Mighty God, Everlasting Father, Prince of Peace, Of the increase of His government and peace there will be no end, upon the throne of David and over His kingdom, to order it and establish it with judgment and justice from that time forward, even forever. The zeal of the Lord of hosts will perform this."

Revelation 21:1-5 "Now I saw **a new heaven and a new earth**, for the first heaven and the first earth had passed away. Also there was no more sea. Then I, John, saw the holy city, New Jerusalem, coming down out of heaven from God, prepared as a bride adorned for her husband. And I heard a loud voice from heaven saying, 'Behold, the tabernacle of God is with men, and He will dwell with them, and they shall be His people. God Himself will be with them and be their God. And God will wipe away every tear from their eyes; there shall be no more death, nor sorrow, nor crying. There shall be no more pain, for the former things have passed away.'

Then He who sat on the throne said. 'Behold, I make all things new.' And He said to me. 'Write, for these words are true and faithful."

John 14:1-6 "'Let not your heart be troubled; you believe in God, believe also in Me. In My Father's house are many mansions; if it were not so, I would have told you. I go to prepare a place for you. And if I go and prepare a place for you, I will come again and receive you to Myself; that where I am, there you may be also. And where I go you know, and the way you know.'

Thomas said to Him, 'Lord, we do not know where You are going, and how can we know the way?'

Jesus said to him, 'I am the way, the truth, and the life. No one comes to the Father except through Me."

Isaiah 55:11 "So shall My word be that goes forth from My mouth; it shall not return to Me void, but it shall accomplish what I please, and it shall prosper in the thing for which I sent it."

Underlining and bold print added for emphasis, italics added for clarity.

CHAPTER 11: THE TESTIMONY OF JESUS

JESUS THE CHRIST'S TESTIMONY TO THE FACT THAT HE FULFILLED OLD TESTAMENT PROPHESY

THE FOURFOLD WITNESS

1. John the Baptizer: John 5:3 l-36a "If I bear witness of Myself, My witness is not true. There is another who bears witness of Me, and I know that the witness which He witnesses of Me is true. You have sent to John, and he has borne witness to the truth. Yet I do not receive testimony from man, but I say these things that you may be saved. He was the burning and shining lamp, and you were willing for a time to rejoice in his light. But I have a greater witness than John's;"

2. His works: John 5:36b "for the works which the Father has given Me to finish-- the very works that I do—bear witness of Me, that the Father has sent Me."

3. The Father's testimony at His baptism by John: John 5:37-38 "And the Father Himself, who sent Me, has testified of Me. You have neither heard His voice at any time, nor seen His form."

4. The Scriptures: John 5:38-40,46-47 "But you do not have His word abiding in you, because whom He sent, Him you do not believe. You search the Scriptures, for in them you think you have eternal life; and these are they which testify of Me. But you are not willing to come to Me that you may have life." 46 "For if you believed Moses, you would believe Me; for he wrote about Me. But if you do not believe his writings, how will you believe My words?" See also Matthew 5:17-18.

IN THE BEGINNING OF HIS MINISTRY after reading the Messianic prophesy in Isaiah 61:1-2 to the people in the synagogue at Nazareth He said, "Today this Scripture is fulfilled in your hearing." Luke 4:21

DURRING HIS ARREST "Then Jesus answered and said to them, 'Have you come out as against a robber, with swords and clubs to take Me? I was daily with you in the temple teaching, and you did not seize Me, but the Scriptures must be fulfilled." Mark 14:48-49.

AFTER HIS RESURECTION on the road to Emmaus to two of His disciples: "Then He said to them, 'O foolish ones, and slow of heart to believe in all that the prophets have spoken! Ought not the Christ to have suffered these things and to enter into His glory?' And beginning at Moses and all the Prophets, He expounded to them in all the Scriptures the things concerning Himself." Luke 24:25-27. Please read the whole account at Luke 24:13-35

BEFORE HIS ASCENSION: Luke 24:44-48 "Then He said to them, 'These are the words which I spoke to you while I was still with you, that all things must be fulfilled which were written in the Law of Moses and the Prophets and the Psalms concerning Me.' And He opened their understanding, that they might comprehend the Scriptures. Then He said to them, 'Thus it is written, and thus it was necessary for the Christ to suffer and to rise from the dead the third day, and that repentance and remission of sins should be preached in His name to all nations, beginning at Jerusalem. And you are witnesses of these things."

CHAPTER 12: MY REDEEMER LIVES!

WHATEVER MAY COME YOUR WAY

It is my prayer that your faith in Jesus the Christ may grow day by day. That wherever the path of life leads you; whether wealth or poverty, health or sickness, family and friends or isolation, you maintain your integrity to God and His principles.

Job has long been the "poster boy" of integrity. His book was written about 1000 years before Jesus Christ walked this earth yet Job had such a strong faith in his Redeemer that no matter what Satan threw at him he never wavered:

Job 19:23-27
"Oh, that my words were written!
Oh, that they were inscribed in a book!
That they were engraved on a rock
With an iron pen and lead, forever!
For I know that my Redeemer lives,
And he shall stand at last on the earth;
And after my skin is destroyed, this I know,
That in my flesh I shall see God,
Whom I shall see for myself,
And my eyes shall behold, and not another.
How my heart yearns within me!"

John 20:30-31

"And truly Jesus did many other signs in the presence of His disciples, which are not written in this book; but these are written that you may believe that Jesus is the Christ, the Son of God, and that believing you may have life in His name."

Apostle John

CHAPTER 13: GENESIS THROUGH REVELATION POINTS TO JESUS

PROPHECY	FULFILLED IN JESUS THE CHRIST
Gen. 5:1-32;11:10-26;Ruth 4:18-22; 1Chr. 1:1-4, 24-27, 34; 2:1-15	Matt. 1:2-16; Luke 3:23-38 Genealogy of Jesus Christ
Isaiah 7:14	Matt. 1:23 virgin birth
Micah 5:2	Matt. 2:6 born in Bethlehem
Hosea 11:1	Matt. 2:15 escape to Egypt
Jeremiah 31:15	Matt. 2:18 massacre of children
Isaiah 40:3	Matt. 3:3; Mark 1:3; John 1:23; John the baptizer
Isaiah 9:1-2	Matt. 4:15-16 His ministry
Isaiah 53:4	Matt. 8:17 He bore our sickness
Malachi 3:1	Matt. 11:10; Mark 1:2; Luke 7:27 messenger
Isaiah 52:1-4	Matt. 12:18-21 behold My Servant
Jonah 1:17	Matt. 12:38-42 death & resurrection
Isaiah 6:9-10; Psalm 78:2	Matt 13:14-15,35; Mark 4:12; Luke8:10; John 12:40
Isaiah 29:13	Matt. 15:8-9; Mark 7:6-7 vain worship
Zechariah 9:9	Matt. 21:5; John 12:15 King is coming
Psalm 118:26	Matt.21:9;Mark11:9-10;Luke19:38; John12:13
Isaiah 56:7; Jeremiah 7:11	Matt.21:13; Mark11:17; Luke19:46 cleans temple
Psalm 8:2	Matt. 21:16 children praise Him
Psalm 118:22-23	Matt.21:42;Mark12:10-11;Luke20:17 cornerstone
Psalm 110:1	Matt 22:44; Mark 12:36;Luke20:42-43
Zechariah 13:7	Matt.26:31;Mark 14:27 sheep will scatter
Jeremiah 32:6-9	Matt. 27:9-10 thirty pieces of silver
Psalm 22:18	Matt. 27 35;John19:24 divided My garments
Psalm 22:1	Matt. 27:46; Mark 15:34 My God, My God,
Isaiah 53:12	Mark15:28; Luke22:37 numbered w/transgressors
Malachi 4:5-6	Luke 1:17 forerunner of the Messiah
Isaiah 40:3-5	Luke 3:4-6 make His paths straight
Isaiah 61:1-2	Luke 4:18-19 anointed to preach
Psalm 31:5	Luke 23:46
Psalm 69:9	John 2:17 "Zeal for Your house has eaten me up."
Isaiah 54:13	John 6:45 "And they shall all be taught by God."
Isaiah 53:1	John 12:38 "Lord, who has believed our report?"
Psalm 41:9	John 13:18 betrayed by a friend
Psalm 68:4	John 15:25 "They hated Me without a cause."
Ex.12:46;Num.9:12;Psalm34:20	John 19:36 no bones broken
Zechariah 12:10	John 19:37 He is pierced

Matthew, Mark and John were eyewitnesses of all of the events they wrote about. Luke was not an eyewitness but had gathered the reports of others. Many of these events are written about by more that one of them. At Deuteronomy 19:15 the law stated, "by the mouth of two or three witnesses the matter shall be established." These are written to show that the apostles and disciples referred back to prophecy to prove that Jesus is the promised Messiah/Christ.

THE SERMONS AND TEACHINGS OF THE APOSTLES

VERSES FROM OLD TESTAMENT	FULFILLED IN JESUS
Psalm 69:25,109:8	Acts 1:20 replacing Judas
Joel 2:28-32;Ps.16:8-l1,l10:1	Acts 2 The Holy Spirit, Peters 1st sermon
Deu.18:15,18,19;Gen.22:18;26:4;28:14	Acts 3 Jesus is the Promised One
Psalm 118:22	Acts 4:1-22 before the Sanhedrin
Psalm 2:1-2	Acts 4:23-31 praying for boldness
Ex.2:14;3:6,15;Deu.18:15;many more	Acts 6-7 Stephen accused of blasphemy
Isaiah 53:7-8	Acts 8:26-40 Philip helps an Ethiopian
Ps. 89:20;2:7; 16:10; 1 Sam. 13:14; Habakkuk 1:5; Isaiah 55:3;49:6	Acts 13:13-52 Paul & friends at Antioch
Amos 9:11-12	Acts 15:6-29 Gentiles turning to God
Isaiah 6:9-10	Acts 28:17-31 Paul's ministry at Rome
Habakkuk 2:4	Romans 1:16-17 the just live by faith
Psalm 62:12; Proverbs 24:12	Rom.2:1-16 God judges by Jesus Christ
Ps.5:9;10:7;14:l-3;36:1;53:l-3;140:3; Ecc.7:20; Isaiah 58:7-8	Rom.3:9-26 the law gave us knowledge of sin, redemption is in Christ Jesus
Genesis l5:5-6;17:5;Ps.32:1-2	Rom.4:l-25 justified by faith in Jesus
Psalm 44:22	Rom.8:31-39 God's everlasting love
Gen.18:10,14;21:12;25:23;Ex.9:16;33:19 Mal.1:2-3;Hosea 1:10;2:23; Isaiah 10:22-23;1:9;8:14;28:16	Rom.9 Israel's rejection of Christ and God's purpose and justice
Lev.18:5;Deu.30: 12-14;32:21 ;Joel2:32 Isaiah28: 16;52:7;53:l ;65:1-2;Ps.19:4; Nahum 1:15	Rom.10 Israel needs the Gospel but rejects it
I Kings 19:10,14,18;Deu.29:4;Ps.69:22 23 Isaiah 29:l0;40:13;59:20-21;Job 41:11 Jeremiah 23:18	Rom.11 Israel's rejection is not total or final
Deu.32:35; Proverbs 25:21-22	Rom. 12 serve God behave like a Christian
Ex.20:13-15,17;Deu.5:17-19,21;Lev.19:18	Rom.13:8-l4 love your neighbor; put on Christ
Isaiah 45:23;11: 10;52:15;Ps.69:9;18:49; 117:1;2Sam.22:50;Deu.32:43	Rom.14-15 Jews &Gentiles glorify God; As Christ received us receive one another
Isaiah 29:14; Jeremiah 9:24	1Cor. 1 Christ= power and wisdom of God
Isaiah 64:4;40:13	1 Cor.2 hidden wisdom of God revealed through His Spirit
Job 5:13; Psalm 94:11	1Cor.3-4 we belong to Christ
Deuteronomy 17:7;19:19;22:21,24;24:7	1Cor.5 purge out evil
Genesis 2:24	lCor,6:12-ch.7 we are one with Christ; flee sexual immorality
Deuteronomy 25:4	1Cor.9 we have not used this right lest we hinder the Gospel of Christ
Many Old Testament examples; Ex.32:6 Ps. 24:1	1Cor. 10 we belong to Christ; flee from idolatry
Ps.8:6;Isa.22:13;25:8;Gen.2:7;Hosea 13:14	1Cor. 15 the risen Christ: our faith, hope and victory

VERSES FROM OLD TESTAMENT	FULFILLED IN JESUS
Psalm 116:10	2Cor.4 we believe and speak, knowing that God will also raise us up with Jesus
Is.49:8;52:11; Lev.26:12;Jer.32:38 Ez.37:27;20:34,41;2Sam.7:14	2Cor.5:17-7:1 become reconciled to God through Christ and be holy
Gen.15:6;12:3;18:18;22:18;26:4;28:14 Deu.27:26;21:23;Lev.l8:5;Hab.2:4 Gen.12:7;13:15;24:7	Gal.3 Christ redeemed us from curse of the Law; Law was tutor to bring us to Christ
Isaiah 54:1;Gen.21:10;Lev.19:18	Gal.4:21-5:26 Jesus made us free love fulfills Law walk in Spirit
Ps.68:18;4:4;Zech.8:16	Eph.4 Christ gave us spiritual gifts, we must walk in the Spirit, do not grieve the Spirit
Deu.25:4;Luke 10:7	1Tim.5:17-20 honor the elders <u>NOTE</u> the quote from Luke shows that Paul considered that Gospel to be Scripture along with the Book of Deuteronomy.
Ps.2:7;97:7;104:4;45:6-7;102:25-27; Ps.l10:1;2Sam.7:14;Deu.32:43	Hebrews I Jesus is exalted above all, worshiped by angels, seated at God's right hand
Ps.8:4-6;22:22;2Sam.22:3;Is.8:17-18	Heb.2 Son was made lower than angels to suffer death, be crowned with glory that He might bring many sons to glory
Ps95:7-11	Heb.3 be faithful, we are partakers of Christ
Ps.95:7,8,11;Gen.2:2	Heb.4:1-13 enter His rest/ mix faith w/gospel we have heard
Psalm 2:7;110:4;Gen,22:17	Heb.4:14-6:20 Jesus is High priest forever; come boldly
Ps.110:4	Heb.7 Jesus made priest forever by oath from God; He became a surety of a better covenant
Ex.25:40;Jer.31:31-34	Heb.8 Jesus is the mediator
Ex.24:8	Heb.9:11-28 Jesus put away sin by the sacrifice of Himself
Ps.40:6-8;Jer.31:33-34;Deu.32:35-36 Habakkuk 2:3-4	Heb.10 His death=God's will; hold fast the confession of our hope; just live by faith
Gen.5:24;21:12 many examples of faith	Heb.11 all these obtained a good testimony through faith, God provided something better for us, that we will be made perfect together

VERSES FROM OLD TESTAMENT	FULFILLED IN JESUS
Prov.3:11-12;Ex.19:12-13;Deu.9:19 Haggai 2:6	Heb. 12 Jesus=author&finisher of faith/ mediator new covenant
Deu.31:6,8;Joshua 1:5; Ps.118:6	Heb. 13 Jesus is the same forever. Do not be swayed by various and strange doctrines.
Ex.20:13-14;Lev.19:18;Deu.5:17-18	James 2:1-13 do not hold the faith of our Lord Jesus Christ with partiality.
Gen.15:6	James 2:14-26 have works with faith
Prov.3:34	James 4 Humble yourselves in the Lord's sight and He will lift you up.
Lev.11:44-45;19:2;20:7;Is.40:6-8	1Pet. 1 We were redeemed by Christ, be holy in conduct.
Is.28:16;8:14;53:9;Ps.118:22	1Pet.2 Christ suffered for us leaving an example to follow
Ps.34:12-16;Is.8:12	1Pet.3 Bless one another; better to suffer for doing good than evil for Christ also suffered, the just for the unjust.
Prov.10:12;11:31	1Pet.4 If you are abused for the name of Christ, blessed are you, for the Spirit of God rests upon you.
Prov.3:34	1Pet.5 Submit to God/resist devil
Prov.26:11	2Pet.2 Returning to a sinful life after knowing Jesus will leave you worse off than to never have known him
Ps.2:9	Rev.2:18-29 "And he who overcomes, and keeps My works until the end, to him I will give power over the nations" vs.26.
Is.22:22	Rev.3:7-13 "Because you have kept My command to persevere, I also will keep you from the hour of trial which shall come upon the whole world, to test those who dwell on the earth." Verse 10.

DISCUSSION STARTERS

TEACHING AND REVIEW QUESTIONS

When asking children the questions, be sure to use words understood by the child. You may need to use the dictionary to make the questions age appropriate or to rephrase the questions so each child will understand.

Introduction

1. How do we know the Bible alone is the word of God? (Page iii)
2. How do we know these so called fulfilled prophesy were not just cleaver guessing on the part of the writer? (Page iii)

Chapter 1

3. What were some of the prophesies of the Messiah that were fulfilled in the birth of Jesus?

Chapter 2

4. Who came in the "spirit and power of Elijah…to make ready a people prepared for the Lord"? (Page 13)

Chapter 3

5. What was prophesied about the ministry of the Messiah?
6. Who are the Gentiles? (Page 27)
7. Was it always Gods intention to bless all the families of the earth through the Messiah? (Pages x, 2, 6)

Chapter 4

8. Was it a friend or an enemy that betrayed Jesus? (Page 28)
9. What significance is the 30 pieces of silver? (Exodus 21:32 pages 28 and 31)
10. Who deserted Jesus? (Page 29)

Chapter 5

11. Who is the mediator of the New Covenant? (Page 32)
12. How did He institute the New Covenant? (Page 32)
13. Why do we call Genesis through Malachi the Old Testament?
14. Why do call Matthew through Revelation the New Testament?

Chapter 6

15. Did Jesus know in advance that He would have to suffer greatly to redeem us from sin and death? (Pages 34 & 35)

16. Did He know He would have to die? (Page 39)

Chapter 7

17. How many years before Jesus died on the cross did King David write Psalm 22? (Page 43)

18. What is so remarkable about Psalm 22? (Page 43)

Chapter 8

19. How do we know that Jesus was brought back to life (resurrected)? (Page 49)

20. What does the resurrection of Jesus mean to us? (Page 51)

Chapter 9

21. What is so unique about Christianity? (Page 52)

22. Is Christianity a religion or a relationship? (Pages 52-54)

23. What is the gift of God and what are some verses that clarify your answer? (Page 52)

24. How do we receive and accept the free gift of God? (Page 54)

25. How do we begin a personal relationship with Jesus? (Page 54)

Chapter 10

26. Who is the king in the Kingdom of God? (Page 55)

27. Where is the Kingdom of God? (Page 55-59)

28. How long will the Kingdom of God rule? (Page 55)

29. Is Jesus ruling now? (Page56)

Chapter 11

30. In John 5:31-47 Jesus names 4 things that testify of Him, what are they? (Page 60)

31. Did Jesus ever refer to the scriptures as being fulfilled in Him? (Page 60)

Chapter 12

32. How did Job maintain his integrity as he suffered all his trials? (Page 61)

33. Matthew, Mark, and Luke had already written their gospels on the life of Jesus, why did John write his account? (Page 61)

Chapter 13

34. Why are there 4 gospels? (Page 62)

35. In Acts 17:6 the Jews that did not believe that Jesus is the Messiah accused His disciples of turning "the world upside down". How did the apostles and disciples convince so many people that Jesus is the long awaited Messiah or Christ? (Pages 63-65)

36. At 1Peter 3:15 we are admonished to "sanctify the Lord God (or Christ as Lord) in your hearts, and always be ready to give a defense to everyone who asks you a reason for the hope that is in you." How should we do that?

ANSWERS TO TEACHING AND REVIEW QUESTIONS

Introduction

1. Fulfilled prophecy is unique to the Bible and found in the Bible alone.

2. The predictions were made between 1500BC and 400BC with explicit detail, no person or persons unaided by Divine inspiration could have done that.

Chapter 1

3. a) Born of a virgin.

   b) A descendant of King David

   c) Born in Bethlehem.

   d) Several others can be mentioned.

Chapter 2

4. John the baptizer.

Chapter 3

5. a) That He would preach liberty to the captives, heal the brokenhearted, and comfort all who morn. (Page 16)

   b) Where He would preach. (Page 17)

   c) He would speak in parables. (Pages 18-19)

   d) He would be a savior, healer and miracle worker. (Pages 20-21)

   e) He would be a prophet like Moses. (Page 22)

   f) He would come riding on a donkey. (Page 23)

   g) He would become a light to the Gentiles. (Page 26)

   h) He WILL restore Israel and establish justice for all. (Pages 26-27

6. Gentiles are anyone that is not an Israelite or Jewish by birth.

7. Yes.

Chapter 4

8. A friend

9. 30 pieces of silver was the price of a slave that had been killed.

10. All of His followers.

Chapter 5

11. Jesus.

12. When He celebrated His last Passover with His disciples He instituted the Lords Supper which we celebrate at Communion.

13. Testament, according to the Dictionary, means covenant. Genesis through Malachi records God's dealings with mankind through His Law based covenant with Israel. In Jeremiah 31:31-34 God said that He would make a "new covenant" and this He did through Jesus.

14. In the Dictionary the word testament in Law is a document by which a person declares his will concerning the disposal of his personal property after his death; a will. Jesus inaugurated the New (grace based) Covenant on the day before He died on the cross for our sins. Please read Hebrews 9:16-28 which calls Jesus' death the death of the "testator" which had to occur to put the New Covenant or Testament in force. The whole book of Hebrews proclaimed the superiority of Jesus and the New Covenant to the old priesthood and the old Law based covenant.

Chapter 6

15. Yes but He came willingly to fulfill all the prophesies. Isaiah wrote of My Servant and the Suffering Servant which is the Messiah and Jesus knew these prophesies applied to Him.

16. Yes but He had full faith that His Father would resurrect Him (bring Him back to life).

Chapter 7

17. 1000 years.

18. a) The Jews did not know about crucifixion, they punished criminals by stoning.
    b) David wrote as if he himself were experiencing the excruciating pain of crucifixion.

    c) Crucifixion was a Roman punishment and the nation of Rome did not exist until several centuries later.

    d) Psalm 22 is so detailed that only an all knowing God could have caused David to write it.

Chapter 8

19. a) He appeared numerous times to His disciples.

b) The same disciples that fled out of fear when He was arrested boldly proclaimed His resurrection and our hope of eternal life through His sacrifice. Many were willing to die for proclaiming Jesus as Lord.

20. a) All the promises of God are certain to be fulfilled.

b) He does not and will not change.

c)All the people of the earth share in the promises of God.

d)The resurrection proves that God accepted Jesus' sacrifice for us.

Chapter9

21. All other religions teach that you can save you by doing certain things. Jesus did all for us and we only have to believe, ask and receive.

22. a) Relationship was what Adam had with God in the Garden of Eden. Jesus Christ as the second Adam (Romans 5:12-17; 1Corinthians 15:20-24,45-49) bought back (redeemed) what Adam lost for the whole human race when he disobeyed God and broke the relationship.

b) Our faith is in the "name (meaning character and authority) of the Father and of the Son and of the Holy Spirit" not in the name of religion. We follow the Bible through the leading of the Holy Spirit not the dictates of a religion, group, organization, society, etc. However we belong to the Body of Christ which operates in unity and harmony through the leading of the Holy Spirit as we live our life under the rule of the Kingdom of God and we are not "lone wolves". See Acts 2:40-47; Hebrews 10:24-25

c) We are adopted as sons and daughters of God. His Spirit bears witness with our spirit that we are the children of God. (Romans 8:14-17) This is a very close relationship, a family relationship.

d) James 1:27 "Pure and undefiled religion before God and the Father is this: to visit orphans and widows in their trouble, and to keep oneself unspotted from the world." Religion that God accepts entails helping those that cannot help themselves. It is a relationship with people.

e)WHAT BRINGS US INTO THAT PERSONAL RELATIONSHIP IS FAITH IN JESUS CHRIST AND HIS SACRIFICE FOR US. WE MUST BE BORN AGAIN. See John 3:1-21: 1Peter 1:22-23.

23. Eternal life through faith in Jesus Christ. John 3:16-18; 6:28-29,37-51

24. a) Confess our sins. Romans 6:23; 1John 1:8-9

   b) Believe in the Lord Jesus Christ. Romans 10:9-10; Ephesians 2:8-9; Acts 4:12

   c) Live by faith. Romans 1:16-17

25. a) We <u>ask</u> Jesus to come into our life.

   b) We <u>believe</u> He died for us and that His blood pays for our sins so we can have   the free gift of eternal life.

   c) By <u>faith</u> we <u>receive</u> that gift.

   d) We <u>acknowledge</u> Jesus as our Lord and Savior.

Chapter 10

26. Jesus.

27. On earth, Daniel said it will consume all kingdoms.

28. Forever.

29. Yes, He is ruling in the midst of His enemies.

Chapter 11

30. a) John the baptizer

   b) The works of Jesus

   c) The Father's testimony at His baptism

   d) The Scriptures

31. Yes, throughout His ministry, at His arrest, after His resurrection and before His ascension.

Chapter 12

32. He knew beyond a shadow of a doubt that his Redeemer lives.

33. "that you may believe that Jesus is the Christ, the Son of God, and that believing you may have life in His name." John 20:31

Chapter 13

34. At Deuteronomy 19:15 the law stated that at the mouth of 2 or 3 witnesses the matter shall be established.

35. They referred back to the Law, Psalms, and Prophets to prove that all these prophesies of the Messiah were fulfilled in Jesus the Christ.

36. a) Show from the Old Testament the prophesies and the New Testament the fulfillment in Jesus Christ.

b) Tell them how Jesus changed your life.

c)Give them a copy of this book.

Biography

I compiled this after my son, Guy Schleicher, died suddenly at the age of 33 of a massive heart attack. I worked on it while my husband, Greg, was being treated for lung cancer. I used the information in it to console and strengthen him when he was dying November of 2010 of brain cancer. My faith was increased through the writing of this book to the point that I can say without reservation "To be absent from the body is to be present with the Lord."

My description of my book is:

Jesus the Christ is the only person in the history of the world whose life was completely foretold from conception to his death on the cross and resurrection. This book was written and illustrated to be used in Sunday schools, Christian Schools, jail and prison ministries, Christian based drug rehabilitation, and home Bible studies. It was written for both the believer and seeker.